MAKE DISCIPLES

MAKE DISCIPLES

Person-to-Person Evangelism Programs

Joel D. Heck

Developed in cooperation with the Board for Evangelism Services, The Lutheran Church—Missouri Synod.

Publishing House
St. Louis

Bible verses so indicated are from the Revised Standard Version of the Bible, copyrighted 1946, 1952, © 1971, 1973. Used by permission.

Scripture quotations marked NIV are from The Holy Bible: NEW INTERNATIONAL VERSION, Copyright © 1978 by the New York International Bible Society. Used by permission of Zondervan Bible Publishers.

Copyright © 1984 Concordia Publishing House
3558 S. Jefferson Avenue, St. Louis, MO 63118
Manufactured in the United States of America

All rights reserved. No part of this publication may be reproduced, stored in a retrieval system, or transmitted, in any form or by any means, electronic, mechanical, photocopying, recording, or otherwise without the prior written permission of Concordia Publishing House.

Library of Congress Cataloging in Publication Data
Heck, Joel D., 1948–
    Make disciples.

    (Speaking the Gospel series)
    1. Evangelistic work. I. Title. II. Series.
BV3790.H382 1984   269'.2   83-27271
ISBN 0-570-03935-5 (pbk.)

---

3 4 5 6 7 8 9 10 IB 93 92 91 90

Contents

Introduction		7
Chapter 1	The Home Visitation Approach	11
Chapter 2	The Correspondence Approach	34
Chapter 3	The Campus Approach	39
Chapter 4	The Educational Approach	59
Chapter 5	The Marketplace Approach	76
Chapter 6	The Mass Meeting Approach	95
Notes		107
Bibliography		110

Introduction

The primary motivation for sharing the Gospel is the indwelling Holy Spirit, and the secondary motivation is what the love of Jesus Christ means personally to the Christian. The attitude that best fosters participation in evangelism activities is a sincere and urgent desire to share with others the Good News of salvation by grace through faith in Jesus Christ. St. Paul says, "For Christ's love compels us, because we are convinced that one died for all...."(2 Cor. 5:14 NIV).

In evangelism, as in any area of congregational life, attitudes are much more important than programs. Without proper attitudes, there is no need for programs. If there is a Biblical attitude toward evangelism in the congregation, well designed and correctly executed programs will help Christians carry out the task our Lord has given us of making disciples of all nations (Matt. 28:18-20). The intent of this book is to acquaint the reader with some of the programs that have helped Christians accomplish the goal of making disciples and some of the principles that underlie those programs.

The programs described in these pages are only a few of the total number of programs that could have been surveyed. The author does not claim this book is exhaustive. However, he has included the major evangelism programs being widely used by Lutherans throughout the United States, as well as some nondenominational programs and resources, with special attention given to those in use in The Lutheran Church—Missouri Synod (LCMS). It is hoped that this book will not only introduce many of the evangelism programs that could be used by individuals and congregations, but that it will also broaden one's view of evangelism and give birth to new and innovative ways in which the Gospel may be shared.

Some congregations will say that everything they do is evangelism. It is not always easy to define what an evangelism program is, because in one sense evangelism occurs every time the Gospel is presented in spoken or written form. Our definition of an evangelism program is an organized effort by members of a Christian congregation to reach non-Christians with the Gospel of Jesus Christ. Some attention will be paid to "internal evangelism," defined as efforts to reach congregational members who have fallen away from Christ.

Media use for evangelism (television, radio, etc.) has been intentionally overlooked for two reasons. First, this book deals with person-to-person evangelism by members of a Christian congregation, and media evangelism does not fit into this category. Second, this field is changing so rapidly that our remarks would be obsolete by the time this book is published.[1]

The book is organized into chapters, based upon the location in which the evangelistic message is spoken. The general word "approach" is used to describe these six styles of evangelism. The titles of the chapters suggest these locations or approaches: face-to-face at the home of the unchurched person, at the home of the unchurched person via the mail, on the high school or college campus, in the small group at the church or in the Christian home, in the marketplace, or in the corporate congregational gathering.

The more specific word "program" is used in each chapter to describe ways in which that particular approach is carried out. In many instances, additional resources are given, which are not described and evaluated, but are simply offered in order to provide the reader with information. While many of the programs included here will be dated or no longer in use in years to come, these six approaches will probably continue until Christ returns.

In each chapter a concrete congregational example is given in order to illustrate that chapter's approach and in order to demonstrate one of the most effective programs for carrying out that approach. These are congregations where that program has been used effectively over a number of years.

The programs mentioned in these pages deal with the process of spiritual birth. They do not include discipleship programs, follow-up programs, internal growth programs (except insofar as they are used in reaching out at the same time), devotional programs, public relations programs, and the like. Covered here are those programs or types of ministries which verbalize the message of salvation by grace through faith in Jesus Christ so that the person hearing the message has an opportunity to embrace Jesus as his or her Savior. We are not concerned with those factors leading up to spiritual birth, nor are we concerned with the events that follow. Pre-evangelism is essential and evangelism without follow-up is spiritual negligence, but evangelism in the narrow sense of the term is the subject of this book.

It is not always easy to fit programs into certain preconccived categories. Some programs could have been listed in more than one chapter. However, it is hoped that the present system of organization will aid the reader in better understanding and evaluating many of the evangelism programs in use today.

As you read, look for programs that provide adequate, Biblically based training. Look for programs that prepare the field before planting the seed of the Gospel. Look for programs that capitalize on the ready influence Christians have with non-Christian friends and relatives. Look for programs that provide relationships. Look for programs that provide thorough follow-up, follow-up that can be monitored. Look for programs that do not merely proclaim the Gospel, but programs that show how the Gospel can meet a personal need. Look for programs that involve many lay people. Look for programs that involve the potential disciple in a small group before becoming a member of the Christian congregation. Look for the program that makes creative use of visual aids.

Chapter 1

The Home Visitation Approach

The programs surveyed in this chapter are those that involve the Christian in going to the home of the non-Christian in order to share the Gospel at the door or in the living room. The first parts of the chapter include those programs that concentrate on making brief contact with the non-Christian during some kind of survey work, while later parts of the chapter have to do with those programs that seek to gain entrance into the home for the purpose of sharing the Gospel in greater depth. Finally, a series of questions are gathered together for use as an evaluation tool for the person who wants to know how effective and theologically sound a particular program is.

Ongoing Ambassadors for Christ

Ongoing Ambassadors for Christ (OAFC) is a program designed to involve high school and college age youth in witness, Bible study, and Christian fellowship, with the primary accent on witnessing about God's gift of salvation in Jesus Christ. The program involves youth from a number of congregations in a given geographical area, each of which hosts an OAFC weekend once or twice a year. The program then rotates from congregation to congregation, one weekend each month, under the leadership of two directors, usually a pastor and a layman.

According to the *OAFC Crier*, the quarterly publication of the organization,

> The Ongoing Ambassadors for Christ movement is an "ongoing"

witnessing program for youth confirmed and up (*sic*) of The Lutheran Church—Missouri Synod. Every month groups bring new recruits to train and to conduct witness surveys. The three-fold goal is to (1) Witness to all of Jesus Christ, our Savior; (2) Find the unchurched for participating congregations; and (3) Train other youth to witness for Christ. The movement is supported by faith, prayer, love, and freewill contributions of interested people.

One of the many areas in which the OAFC program is very active in the United States is southern Indiana, where activity began in 1975. One of the area directors is the Rev. J. V. Moyer, pastor of St. Peter's Lutheran Church in Brownstown.

"I was very wary of the program at first," Pastor Moyer admits. "I was concerned that it would not just appeal to the whims of youth, but would really be an evangelism program. Indeed it was, and it is. The youth are simply thrilled at the power that God puts in them by simply following the evangelism methods of OAFC."

"Our congregation is also enthusiastic about the program," Pastor Moyer said. "They always respond positively to the youth as they praise God in our worship services, and as they talk about their experiences in calling and about the results of their calls. Many youth of our congregation, who have gone through the program, are either training for or are seriously considering entering one of the professional ministries of our church."

The strength of OAFC in recruiting young people for full-time church work has been emphasized by Dr. Kent Hunter of the Church Growth Analysis and Learning Center in a 1980 report on the movement. Concerning that fact he writes, "Recruiting people for full-time church work is a phenomenally successful experience for young people involved in OAFC."[1]

During the weekend experience, youth spend three and a half hours on Saturday in the community, going door-to-door conducting a witness survey. In addition to gaining information about the church affiliation of the people they meet, youth also make use of several basic witnessing methods to share their faith in Jesus Christ. That evening they use their abilities in personal witness, testimony, and song to share with the residents of an area nursing home. The same skills are utilized in the congregation's worship services on Sunday, as well as during a congregational potluck that noon to conclude the weekend.

Dean Blackwell, a layman who assists Pastor Moyer in directing the program, says "Participation in OAFC has provided me with a vehicle to involve and enrich my children in Christian growth, evangelism, and service. It has also helped my wife and me to grow spiritually. In our congregation, the program has encouraged some older members to make evangelism calls, and has increased evangelism and mission awareness."

"I know of no other program that really captivates youth in such a way and really deepens their personal faith," Pastor Moyer says.

The organization traces its beginnings to participation in the Ambassadors for Christ program of the LCMS, a program also surveyed in this chapter. In the interest of sustaining the enthusiasm begun in the Ambassadors for Christ program, an ongoing emphasis was thought necessary. The first OAFC weekend took place in Brownsdale, Minnesota, on June 27, 1970, and the movement mushroomed from there. It was incorporated less than two years later, on March 2, 1972. The Rev. Fred C. Darkow was called as executive director of the organization, now located at 1302 East 7th, Winfield, Kansas 67156.

Since that small beginning, OAFC has conducted programs in nearly every state in the Union and nearly every District in the LCMS. Approximately 20,000 youth have been trained in the witnessing methods of OAFC, and hundreds of thousands of visits have been made by those young people.

The annual highlight of OAFC is the summer training that is held each year, either at the Winfield headquarters or at some host congregation. About 200 youth and several dozen adults bring their enthusiasm, their guitars, their OAFC experiences, and their love for Jesus. They undergo a week of intensive training in preparation for the traveling teams of 8 to 12 young people and one director, which will be sent out at the conclusion of the training sessions. These teams travel to various parts of the country with the intention of beginning another OAFC program or otherwise being of service to congregations in their evangelism ministry.

This writer still vividly recalls a 12-day, 5,200 mile trip in the summer of 1979 with 11 young people. The trip began at Zion Lutheran Church, Fort Wayne, Indiana, the site of that summer's training week, took us to Roseburg, Oregon, on the west coast, and brought us back again to Fort Wayne.

The 11 youth and one director packed themselves and their suitcases into a 15-passenger van, stopping each evening of the trip for a program of singing, Bible study, drama, personal testimony, and witness at a Lutheran church. The closeness that was developed will never be forgotten, and, for some of the team members, still exists. The common goal of sharing Jesus as Savior united all members of that team, particularly as they participated in the worship life and activities of St. Paul's Lutheran Church, Roseburg, Oregon, over the weekend.

Bible study and prayer time punctuated portions of the long days of driving. Dramas were rehearsed en route, and songs were practiced again and again in order to prepare the best possible witness. Gracious hosts received us each night after the evening program at their church, providing meals and lodging for each person. A gracious Savior sustained us and drew us closer to Him.

Other innovative types of ministries have been one of the earmarks of OAFC. A college-age traveling team has provided the same summer experience that we had, but during the nine months of the school year. Couples teams have served in various localities during the summer months. Lutheran youth in Hong Kong and the Philippines got a taste of OAFC during the summer of 1976, through a grant from the Lutheran Women's Missionary League.

Now a listed service organization of the LCMS, OAFC continues to be served by Rev. Darkow, executive director, Mr. Richard Meyer, treasurer, and other part-time staff.

Ambassadors for Christ

Ambassadors for Christ (AFC) is a training program for high school age youth. The young people meet at a specific congregation for an entire weekend, during which they are involved in Bible study, worship, recreation, and training in witnessing.

As a part of the weekend experience, the young people go out into the community in order to witness to their Savior, either from house to house, or at specific homes designated by the host congregation. As a result of this experience, the ambassadors see the Holy Spirit in action through God's Word and discover the thrill of giving testimony to their Savior. Many youth attend quite a number of AFC events, since the weekend is an exciting Christian experience. Some are motivated to pursue a full-time Christian vocation in order to serve their Lord in professional church work.

Participants in the weekend furnish their own transportation to and from the host congregation, but the congregation takes care of all other costs and arrangements. Young people are recruited by a general mailing that is sent to the pastors of congregations in the general area of the host congregation. The pastor is asked to post publicity and personally to recruit young people.

The program is carried out by some of the districts of the LCMS, either through their Board of Evangelism, Board of Youth Ministry, or both, with the assistance of the district executives. Congregations become host congregations by making such a request to the appropriate people. Unlike the monthly activities of OAFC, AFC weekends occur once or twice each year in a given geographical area. While they do not sustain the enthusiasm of the youth in the way that OAFC does, they provide many more youth with the opportunity to participate than can be accommodated by the regional OAFC programs.

Various campuses of LCMS colleges and seminaries have used similar programs to provide evangelism training for the post-high school age. Individual congregations will want to encourage as many youth as possible to attend an AFC weekend, because of the spiritual growth that occurs and because of the training in witnessing that is received.[2]

Community Survey

Variations among community surveys are endless. Almost every congregation has conducted surveys at one time or another with a variety of tools and methods. One such program within the LCMS is "Venture Into Community," in which a survey of the needs of the community is coupled with a Christian witness to Jesus Christ.[3]

One tool for survey use is the "Personal Religious Opinionaire," (*sic*) described in Chapter 16 of the Rev. W. Leroy Biesenthal's *Dialog Evangelism* notebook (see below). A sample of the form to be used is given in the notebook along with instructions on how to use it. The same is true of Kennedy's *Evangelism Explosion* (revised edition), which contains a chapter entitled "Questionnaire Evangelism."[4] The *Evangelism Resource Book* (ERB) also has two pages devoted to "A Community Witness Survey," cf. Book 4. C. There is not enough space in this book to include every resource available in this area, but the above samples should be sufficient for the needs of most congregations.

Scripture Distribution

People who take seriously the belief that the Holy Spirit brings people to faith through God's Word may want to provide homes in their community with Scripture portions, Bibles, or New Testaments. Some people may not allow a church member to come into their home and talk about Jesus Christ, but they will accept a Scripture portion and perhaps read it.

The most remarkable Scripture distribution organization is the Gideons International, with headquarters at 2900 Lebanon Rd., Nashville, Tennessee 37214. The Gideons are well known for placing Bibles in hotels and motels, but not many are aware that the Gideons have placed millions of copies at colleges, universities, and at public and private schools. They have distributed Scripture in hospitals, prisons, jails, and among men and women of the armed forces. In 1983, the total number of Scriptures that the Gideons have distributed worldwide since the inception of the organization passed the 300 million mark. The annual distribution number continues to increase at an accelerated pace.

A Christian organization that works especially with congregations is the World Home Bible League, 16801 Van Dam Rd., South Holland, Illinois 60473. The Canadian Home Bible League is located at Box 524, Station A, Weston, Ontario M9N 3N3. They publish the Gospel of John or other Scripture portions with a customized cover featuring the congregation that distributes them. A congregation can place a portion of the Bible in every home in their community for a very low cost. Scripture portions are available with special markings to assist the reader in finding passages related to salvation. Scripture portions are also available in Spanish, Portuguese, Chinese, and Arabic.

The American Bible Society, copyright owner of the Good News Bible (Today's English Version), is also quite active in Scripture distribution at the lowest possible cost. Founded in 1816, the Society offers a variety of translations of God's Word for congregational use and distribution, in addition to a variety of other helpful tools to assist congregations in their evangelistic outreach. They are located at 1865 Broadway, New York, New York 10023.

Another similar organization is the New York International Bible Society, 144 Tices Lane, East Brunswick, New Jersey 08816. Founded in 1809, this organization seeks to make Bibles, testaments, and Scripture portions available at low cost for teaching purposes, Scripture distribution, and evangelistic outreach.

Other societies and agencies are also involved in such a ministry of Scripture distribution. Many congregations have developed their own method of marking Scripture portions with the plan of salvation (cf. a sample marking, ERB, Book 14. E).

Congregations that wish to attempt to reach apartment dwellers might consider Scripture distribution. Any congregation involved in its community and actively making visits on the unchurched will benefit from the placement of the Word of God in each home and from the wave of positive publicity for their church that accompanies the distribution. The customized covers for the Gospel of John, available from the World Home Bible League, help the community to identify your church as the sponsor of this distribution effort.

Congregations not involved with their community in any other form of evangelistic outreach and public relations ought not to expect to see many results from Scripture distribution. Congregations that include a personal witness at the time of distribution will increase the effectiveness of this program, particularly if names of interested people are taken at the time of the witness.

We now turn our attention to programs that seek to *gain entrance into the home,* to meet people "in the living room."

Evangelism Explosion

Walden, New York, is a small town with a population of approximately 5,000, located 50 miles northwest of New York City. In that predominantly Roman Catholic community, Trinity Lutheran Church was begun in 1959. Since the population of Walden is static, the growth of the congregation is significant. Most of the Protestant churches in Walden show little or no growth. Part of Trinity's growth may be attributed to participation in the Evangelism Explosion program (E.E.), the major thrust of the evangelism ministry of Evangelism Explosion III International, P.O. Box 23820, Ft. Lauderdale, Florida 33307.

The beginnings of Trinity's involvement in visitation evangelism may be traced to a spiritual renewal that took place in the congregation in 1972, two years after the arrival of Pastor Ray Cummings, current senior pastor of Trinity. Increased involvement in Bible study, greater church attendance, and additional financial support were some of the results. A growing interest in and enthusiasm for the mission of the church led eventually to an evangelism visitation program.

Also in 1972, the Rev. Bob Griffin and family moved into the area. An LCMS clergyman, Rev. Griffin was then serving as a full-time evangelist for the Lutheran Evangelistic Movement (a ministry surveyed in Chapter V of this book). In the fall of 1973, Griffin attended an Evangelism Explosion clinic at Coral Ridge Presbyterian Church, Fort Lauderdale, Florida. Thereafter, Rev. Griffin offered to train some of the members of Trinity in the principles and methods he had learned.

After initial successful efforts, Bob Griffin was installed at Trinity in 1979 as evangelist, dividing his work between the congregation and the Lutheran Evangelistic Movement. In the meantime, further training had been undertaken by Rev. Griffin at Fort Lauderdale, along with lay person Fred Walton.

As a result of contacts with E.E. III International, interest in having a small town E.E. clinic grew. Until the late 1970s, all E.E. clinics, first begun in 1967, had been conducted in large churches and in large population areas for various logistical reasons. However, the need was also seen for pastors from smaller communities to have a training experience in a small town church, where a successful E.E. ministry was taking place. After a visit from Archie Parrish, then minister of evangelism at Coral Ridge Presbyterian Church and executive director of E.E. III International, Trinity became a clinic base for four E.E. clinics, beginning in 1979.

While some modification of the program as a result of the small town atmosphere has been encouraged by E.E. III, the congregation follows the E.E. program closely. Trainees undergo a 17-week training program under the supervision of a teacher trainer and a trainer. The trainer takes the trainee out on evangelism calls, while the teacher trainer teaches the actual training sessions. There are six teacher trainers at Trinity, four lay people and the two pastors, in addition to 20 active callers. The basic text for the training is *Evangelism Explosion*, revised edition, by D. James Kennedy, pastor of Coral Ridge Presbyterian Church. A minimum of 15 calls are made with the trainer during the 17-week program. Trainees do weekly homework assignments that include Scripture memorization and the learning of a Gospel presentation, and they are involved in the follow-up that takes place. Those who complete the training cycle are encouraged to become a trainer for another 17 weeks.

While there has not been an explosion of growth at Trinity, Walden, there has been growth, both internal and external. The congregation numbered 365 baptized members and 230 communicants in 1972. Ten years later there were 612 baptized members and 385 communicant members.

Many of the internal activities of the church are designed to complement the external, or outreach, activities of Trinity. A small group program under the leadership of the elders of the congregation helps assimilate new members and involve everyone. Some lay people have been trained to counsel with those who have problems, with particular emphasis on helping new members won through evangelism. "There is a high degree of willingness to invite family, friends, and neighbors to worship," states Pastor Cummings, and "those who have had evangelism training seem to have a better understanding of what the church is all about, its mission and its purpose." Visitors frequently comment about the friendliness of the congregation. A greater sensitivity to the needs of the community, common in evangelistic congregations, is in evidence here.

In short, E.E. has influenced the entire fabric of the congregational life. Even those not directly involved in the E.E. program have a positive feeling about their congregation and its outreach in evangelism. They enhance the effectiveness of the ministry in many ways. Furthermore,

Trinity has helped several other congregations in the surrounding communities to establish an evangelism visitation program in their church.

Lay leader and teacher trainer Fred Walton comments, "E.E. provided me with a clear, concise method of presenting the Gospel. . . . My own relationship to Christ seemed to come into sharper focus. It also provided a method of training others to be effective witnesses. Not only am I able to win souls, I am able to train soul-winners."

Pastor Cummings echoes these thoughts: "The laity is the untapped resource of the church. The need of the hour is expressed in Ephesians 4:12. Pastors are to 'equip the saints for the work of ministry.'. . . Evangelism Explosion is one of the best tools available for that purpose."

Dialog Evangelism

The Rev. W. Leroy Biesenthal, associate secretary for evangelism for the Board for Evangelism Services of the LCMS, is the author of a workbook called *Dialog Evangelism*. The title of the workbook is significant, as the author himself writes:

> The method presented in this workbook is called *Dialog Evangelism* because it seeks to share the Gospel in dialog with persons whom one meets or visits. The method is not "proclaiming" or "declaiming" in a one way conversation. . .but rather a somewhat directed conversation which grows out of the Christian's desire to share the Good News with someone at that point in life and understanding which best suits the situation.[5]

Dialog Evangelism is a 16-week experience with on-the-job training as one of its key features. Homework assignments, classroom teaching and discussion, and actual visitation are combined for the purpose of training Christians more effectively to share their faith in Jesus Christ. One helpful component of the workbook, which enables it to be used on several different levels, is the three sets of worksheets. Persons who are involved in their second or third 16-week evangelism training cycle can use a different set of study questions each time.

While Rev. Biesenthal acknowledges his debt to D. James Kennedy, he charts a distinctive course in evangelism training with some emphasis from the field of Church Growth, concentration on several key theological concepts, and an accent on preparing the field for evangelism.

Among the key theological concepts discussed are the work of the Holy Spirit in bringing about a conversion through the Word, the total depravity of man, the necessity of repentance, and the power of the resurrection of Jesus Christ. The importance of pre-evangelism is stressed in the distinction between Track One and Track Two evangelism. Track One evangelism consists of all those contacts that a congregation has with its community that make the congregation known to the community, apart from the actual sharing of the Gospel with people during Dialog Evangelism. It includes those witness situations that arise spontaneously in the normal activity of daily life. Track Two evangelism consists of visitation evangelism for the purpose of in depth presentation of the Gospel. When Track Two is not producing results, Biesenthal suggests, one reason may be that the congregation is doing little work in Track One evangelism. Sharing the Gospel cannot be done in a vacuum, at least not with any degree of effectiveness.

Biesenthal has changed Kennedy's outline of the Gospel presentation in order to reflect a more precise Biblical theology. For example, where Kennedy calls the second and third parts of his outline "The Gospel" and "The Commitment," Biesenthal calls them "The Message" and "The Response." "The Message" is a better heading, since the second section actually includes both Law and Gospel. "The Response" is better than "The Commitment," since the word "commitment" suggests that the natural man does receive the things of the Spirit of God and that he can cooperate in his own salvation, if only in the decision-making process (contrary to 1 Cor. 2:14 and other passages). The word "response" suggests that the third section of the outline deals with the response of a faith which is now present as a result of the work of the Holy Spirit. It further recognizes that there are a variety of responses that the person may give, including rejection.

One other significant change is the transfer of the "Grace" portion of Kennedy's outline from the second major part of his outline to a transitional statement, which serves as a bridge from "The Introduction" to "The Message." The word "grace" can be misleading in Kennedy's outline, since only the fact that heaven is a free gift is shared there, not the riches of God's grace in Jesus Christ at the cross and the empty tomb. The content of the "Grace" section actually serves as a transition to the presentation of the Law and the Gospel.

While *Dialog Evangelism* is intended for a wide audience, it is especially helpful as a resource book and training manual for pastors and seminary students. Some pastors and lay people, who have used the workbook, have suggested that the assignment schedule needs to be simplified, particularly for the new trainee, by providing specific directions from week to week about which portion of the presentation to prepare and be ready to present.

The workbook, No. 1410, is available from Concordia Publishing House, and a set of 12 teaching cassettes is available from Master Productions, Route 1, Box 66, Cozad, Nebraska 69130. A set of video tapes of Rev. Biesenthal teaching a clinic is available from Rev. Dennis Tegtmeier, First Lutheran Church, 4th and Washington, Papillion, Nebraska 68046.

Making Disciples

Another evangelism program was developed by the Rev. Donald F. Ginkel during the time he served as pastor of Shepherd of the Valley Lutheran Church in West Des Moines, Iowa. His evangelism training workbook is called *Making Disciples: A Guide on How To*. While Dialog Evangelism provides all of the necessary reading material in its notebook, *Making Disciples* is written to be used in conjunction with Kennedy's *Evangelism Explosion*. This course follows rather closely the contents of Kennedy's book. Trainees learn the outline as Kennedy has written it, and they do reading assignments from both Kennedy and Ginkel.

One of the strengths of this program is its Phase I and Phase II training series. Phase I is a series of assignments designed for the new trainee, while Phase II provides assignments for those who have already been trained in visitation evangelism through Phase I. Phase II uses Howard Hendrick's book *Say It With Love* as the basic text in place of Kennedy's book.

Among the distinctive emphases of this program are its very practical assignments, which lead the trainee step by step through the memorization and fleshing out of the Gospel outline. A page containing helpful suggestions about Scripture memorization is included in this study guide, and there is a method for marking a New Testament with God's plan of salvation. The use of a newcomers calling program and a praying hands mold as a gift to new arrivals in the community are also described. Materials may be ordered from Rev. Donald F. Ginkel, 10624 W. 115th Street, Overland Park, KS 66210.

Speaking of Salvation

This evangelism visitation program is an approach that incorporates many of the commonly accepted methods of evangelism training in a distinctively Lutheran approach. Based on the twin poles of repentance and forgiveness stressed by Christ to His disciples in Luke 24:47, "Speaking of Salvation" offers confrontational evangelism training built around a presentation of Law and Gospel.

Weekly training sessions, weekly visits, homework assignments, and prayer are all a part of the regular schedule for participants. Every evangelism visitation program that intends to present the Gospel in the living room has these features.

The outline of the Gospel presentation reflects the author's familiarity with *Evangelism Explosion*. There are three major sections: introduction, presentation, and outcomes. In the introduction, two simple questions are used to lead the person being visited to consider his understanding of eternal life and whether he has a place in heaven. This friendly questioning occurs only after an appropriate amount of time has been devoted to establishing good rapport. The two questions are these: Are you sure of eternal life with God in heaven? Why should God let you into His heaven?

After the introductory part of the visit, the conversation is guided into a discussion of the Biblical message under two main points: Law and Gospel. Every Lutheran and many who are not Lutheran will appreciate this presentation of the message. Under the Law section, the person being visited is acquainted with the Biblical teaching about sin (both original sin and actual sin), the punishment of that sin, and the need for repentance. During the presentation of the Gospel, the evangelist talks about forgiveness of sins made possible by Jesus Christ and received only by faith.

This clear outline emphasizes the fact that only when a person sees his need for forgiveness will he be ready for the sweetness of the Gospel. Emphasis is placed upon the work of the Holy Spirit to bring about saving faith. The significance of the resurrection of Christ is also explained.

So far as it can be humanly done, the presenter will strive to determine if his new friend can show evidence of Christian faith in response to the presentation. The person is then invited to confess that faith in Christ by answering a series of confession questions, questions that are really only a review of the presentation just completed. In this way, the evangelist avoids giving the impression that faith is something you accomplish through prayer. If the answers to the questions give reason to assume that there is now faith in Jesus, then the new Christian will be encouraged to live that faith.

According to the author, there are two possible outcomes of the visit: confession of faith in Jesus Christ and commitment of life. Biesenthal has shown that there are many more possible outcomes, most of which fall short of genuine faith. The author would certainly not deny this. Rather, his intention is to separate these outcomes so that justification and sanctification, Law and Gospel, are not mixed. Thereby one avoids suggesting that man cooperates in achieving his salvation. Many evangelism programs suggest to the person being visited, "Now if you become a Christian, you will of course do this and this and this." "Speaking of Salvation" avoids that mixing of Law and Gospel.

A strong emphasis is placed upon continuation through follow-up. The evangelist will do everything possible to help his new friend become a faithful disciple of Jesus Christ.

The Speaking of Salvation manual includes several additional features that help make it practical. It has an entire chapter on follow-up, a discussion of various "do's and don'ts," a discussion of some of the obstacles that might be confronted during a visit, and a complete outline of assignments for the training period. In order to undergird the author's careful delineation of Law and Gospel, there are several pages devoted to a theological discussion of conversion. Study cards are available with the manual, so that the entire presentation can be easily studied and reviewed. Copies of various record-keeping materials are also included.

Individual copies of the manual are no longer available, but congregations may write for a master copy of the manual for a small fee. They may then make a number of copies for their own use and return the master copy. Write to the author, Rev. Stephen J. Biegel, Our Savior Lutheran Church, P.O. Box 50073, Billings, Montana 59105.

Talk About the Savior

The tremendous influence of D. James Kennedy on evangelism in the Christian churches of America can be seen when program after program of visitation evangelism is patterned after his techniques. The program produced by the Commission on Evangelism of the Wisconsin Evangelical Lutheran Synod (WELS) is no exception.

"Talk About the Savior" is a 16-week program of study and memorization, on the job training, classroom time, and prayer, intended to be used in conjunction with several booklets prepared for that purpose.

The outline of the presentation consists of five main points, which follow roughly the sequence that Kennedy describes. They are, in order: introduce yourself, get acquainted, present sin and grace, seek responses, and close the visit. The two questions of Kennedy have been rewritten in this form: If you died today, do you know for sure where you would be? If you died today and God asked you, "Why should I let you into heaven?", what would you say?

The actual presentation of the message follows a clear Law-Gospel sequence: I. No everlasting life by works; II. God provided everlasting life; and III. By faith everlasting life is ours. Care is taken in the training manual and booklets to avoid any suggestion of man's cooperation in his salvation. "Response" is the word used where Kennedy uses "Commitment." Emphasis is placed upon the work of the Holy Spirit in moving a person to trust in Christ as his Savior.

One of the features in this manual has become quite commonplace in such training manuals. The manual has a chapter containing a model presentation by a trainer, accompanied by his two trainees to a prospect's home. Those who have read other such presentations will find the reading a bit rough. Transitions are not always smooth, and the typesetting does not indicate when the conversation moves from one person to another. However, one will come upon some helpful illustrations in the presentation and gain some new ideas about communicating the Gospel. The presenter is careful not to mix Law and Gospel, particularly in the "Response" portion of the presentation.

The manual contains the assignments for all 16 weeks of the program and includes a brief section on how to recruit trainees. It is available from The Evangelism Bookshop, 2537 W. Oakwood Rd., Oak Creek, Wisconsin 53154.

Gospel Communication Clinic

A Gospel Communication Clinic (GCC) and all of the remaining visitation programs surveyed in this chapter differ from the preceding programs in that they are not based on the 16-week, on the job training model that involves study, classroom time, and actual visitation.

A GCC is a tool designed to help Christians develop their own words for communicating the Gospel in a warm, personal, and practical manner to some friend or relative. Designed by Pastors Paul M. Schmidt and David M. Belasic and published jointly by the Evangelism and Youth Departments of the LCMS, a GCC is an eight-and-a-half hour clinic, usually scheduled for a Friday evening and Saturday.

The clinic involves 20 to 30 people and is geared for both youth and adults. It is an inductive method that helps participants develop their own presentation of the Gospel and write it down so that it can be shared later. Actual visitation does not happen at the clinic, although some role playing does occur. It is hoped that Christians will be motivated to witness to their special friend after the clinic is over.

The GCC is to be led by two carefully prepared leaders. It can be used in a retreat setting or in a church, by individual parishes or a group of parishes.

During the clinic the leaders help participants deal with their fears of witnessing, focus on one particular friend, and develop a Gospel presentation based on that person's needs. Some discussion time is given to the subject of creating opportunities to share the Gospel. Scripture study undergirds this entire process. Most Districts of the LCMS have a list of trained leaders. Materials are available from Concordia Publishing House (CPH), 3558 S. Jefferson Ave., St. Louis, Missouri 63118.

The Touch of His Hand

The World Home Bible League has produced a series of booklets and four color filmstrips called "The Touch of His Hand," which communicate the Gospel through the printed page, the spoken word, and a filmstrip. Discussion time is built into the presentations according to the inductive method.

The first filmstrip discusses the nature of the Bible; the second is about the existence of God; the third deals with suffering and the problem of evil; the fourth shows a person how to become a Christian and remain one.

Participants read verses from the Bible during the course of this series, with the amount of Scripture references gradually increasing during the series of filmstrips. Each filmstrip has two or three parts devoted purely to viewing and a corresponding two or three parts devoted to review and discussion.

"The Touch of His Hand" can be used by itself in a congregational evangelism program, as a follow-up tool for a congregation involved in an evangelism visitation program, or as an inreach tool for reaching inactive members. It may be purchased from The World Home Bible League, 16801 Van Dam Road, South Holland, Illinois 60473 or The Canadian Home Bible League, Box 524, Station A, Weston, Ontario M9N 3N3.

Evangelism Saturation

Parish Leadership Seminars, Inc., (PLS) is a multifaceted organization, which seeks to provide administrative and program helps to Lutheran congregations. These helps are all closely related to the Great Commission. According to the Rev. Donald A. Abdon, founder and executive director of PLS, "Evangelism *is* the abiding mission of the Church in the world..."[6]

PLS offers a program entitled "Evangelism Saturation." It is available in a six-tape series with an accompanying booklet and may be presented in lecture form. This evangelism program makes use of a Gospel presentation adapted slightly from Kennedy, other materials, and practical experience. Strong emphasis is placed on the fact that the

Gospel alone wins men and women to Jesus Christ and that the Gospel alone properly motivates Christians to share their faith.

One advantage of this program is that it provides a simple yet complete package for training lay people in evangelism. Another advantage is the emphasis placed upon personal recruiting by the pastor. Among its disadvantages are that it does not include on the job training and that it does not produce ongoing results. PLS is located at 5601 S. Meridian St., Suite B, Indianapolis, Indiana 46217.

Resources

Among the many resources that could be listed, a few are particularly noteworthy. *Agape Evangelism* (Tyndale) is a book written by a Missouri Synod layman, Richard Korthals, based on his extensive involvement as a full-time lay evangelist for the Michigan District, training lay people in the visitation evangelism approach presented in *Evangelism Explosion*, by D. James Kennedy. It is reviewed in the December, 1980, issue (Vol. 2, No. 2) of *The Evangel-Gram*. It may be ordered directly from the author at P.O. Box 135, Arcadia, Michigan 49613.

Presenting the Gospel (Board for Evangelism) is written by Armand Ulbrich, the original editor of the *Evangelism Resource Book*. It contains most of what is needed to start an evangelism visitation program, although one might wish to see more of the nuts and bolts material, e.g., recruitment of trainees. It is simple, practical, and clear. There are weekly assignments for trainees at the end of each chapter, along with discussion questions and instructions for the training meeting each week.

The book contains excellent material on motivation for evangelism. It is strong in providing helps for the initial light conversation of a visit, sound in its theology, and helpful in explaining what to talk about on follow-up calls. A suggested outline for a Gospel presentation is given in the book, but the trainee develops his own outline and presentation during the training course. A tract entitled "Do You Know?," which uses the author's outline, is available from the Board for Evangelism Services of the LCMS. The author is obviously familiar with Kennedy, but his theological orientation is Lutheran. In some instances, the theology may be too difficult for the average layperson to understand. The book is available at CPH.

The Church in the Community (Eerdmans) is authored by Arthur Graf, parish pastor and former Concordia Seminary professor at Springfield, Illinois. The book provides helpful techniques for enlisting lay people for evangelism and provides material for use in their training.

Described in its pages is an ongoing evangelism program that seeks to reach prospects, inactive members, new members, and visitors at worship services and Sunday school. The opening chapters place emphasis upon the proper motivation and theological basis for evangelism.

The program outlined in this book is known as "The Kingdom Workers Plan." Unfortunately, this book was written before Kennedy made on the job training an important principle for most visitation evangelism programs. Graf's book reminds us, however, that evangelism can happen without on the job training.

Charles Mueller, an LCMS pastor, is the author of *The Strategy of Evangelism* (CPH). Although published in 1965, the book is still well worth reading.

Two programs from the American Lutheran Church (ALC) deserve mention here. "An Evangel for Everyone" is described in the literature as an in-depth, 15-session training program for those people involved in the evangelism visitation program of a congregation. "Training Parish Callers" by Donn L. Rosenauer is developed from the theological base of Baptism as an entry into the Christian family. It is a simple guide for equipping people to listen and respond appropriately with the Gospel. Both programs are available through Augsburg Publishing House, 426 S. Fifth St., Minneapolis, Minnesota 55415.

Readers should also note "How to Visit," an eight-page folder from CPH containing in outline form instructions for people who visit homes in their parish or community, No. 9R2206. Book 5 of the ERB is entitled "Training Witnesses."

An Evaluation Tool

Any congregation truly interested in evangelism will also be interested in evaluating its evangelism programs. Evaluation is not an easy task, but the following pages make an attempt to suggest some methods. A series of questions are provided for the reader to keep in mind as he considers initiating a particular program, or as he evaluates the program or programs that are currently in operation in his congregation. A sample evaluation of one evangelism program is provided at the conclusion of this section. The questions for evaluation purposes are provided in four areas: theology, objectives of the program, effectiveness, and efficiency.[7]

Theology: This category deals with the appropriateness of the theological content of a particular evangelism program.

1. *Is the motivation for evangelism in this program provided by the Gospel?* Poor motivation can come from the desire to build a

large congregation, the need to be successful, or a host of other unsatisfactory reasons.
2. *Are people perceived as persons with real needs, or as "objects" to be evangelized?* When the person being visited is perceived as one with genuine needs, the sharing of the Gospel will be preceded by some careful listening. The presentation will be modified to speak to the needs of that hearer.
3. *Is salvation through faith in Jesus Christ alone a central part of the presentation?*
4. *Are both actual and original sin stressed?* One need not use these theological terms, but the seriousness of sin is less clearly presented when sin is described as a mere collection of wrong actions. After all, everybody makes mistakes.
5. *Is conversion treated as the work of the Holy Spirit and not the decision or work of man?* God does the work of converting, not man, cf. 1 Cor. 2:14, Eph. 2:4-5, John 5:24-26. Man cannot even decide that he wants to be converted.
6. *Is repentance explained and emphasized during the presentation?* The Law must do its work of bringing the sinner to despair of his own goodness and to be genuinely sorry for his sins.
7. *Is conversion seen as just the beginning of one's spiritual life, i.e., is follow-up sufficiently emphasized?*
8. *Is prayer neither ignored in this program nor described as a means of grace?* Prayer partners are helpful, and beginning every activity with prayer is necessary. However, a person is not saved by prayer through faith, but by grace through faith. God may bring about a conversion by His grace while a person is praying, but more often the prayer will express what God has already accomplished.
9. *Is the proper distinction between Law and Gospel maintained?* Here one is concerned about an overemphasis upon either part of the message, about not insisting on obedience to the Law as a part of one's conversion, etc.

Objectives: This category discusses the stated objectives of a program. It also deals with the capability of a program to reach those objectives.
1. *Does the program say exactly who is to be reached?* What is the target population? One cannot expect to reach apartment dwellers by means of a program designed for retirees.
2. *Does the program clearly define the trainees?* For example,

are the trainees youth, every Christian, Christians with the gift of evangelism, etc.?
3. *Does the program say what knowledge will be gained, what attitudes will be changed, and what skills will be developed by participants?*
4. *Is the method of training clearly defined, and are action steps for participants clearly specified?* Do trainees know exactly what they have to do from week to week?
5. *Does the program explain the nature and amount of time, talent, and treasure needed from the congregation and from the participants?*
6. *Are goals suggested for number of trainees, number of calls, number of new members, etc.?*
7. *Is Scripture study by participants an essential ingredient in the training process?*

Effectiveness: This category discusses whether or not the objectives of the program have been reached.
1. *Does the program have a good reputation for accomplishing its stated objectives in congregations where it has been used?*
2. *Is this reputation based on congregational use of the program without major changes or adaptations?* Large-scale changes in the original programs by a local congregation may be responsible for the results obtained in that place.
3. *Does the program emphasize and provide for periodic reevaluation concerning the degree to which the objectives of the program are being or have been achieved?*
4. *Is the program well coordinated with other congregational programs?* For example, sometimes an evangelism program does not work well, because no pre-evangelism is taking place in the community.
5. *Is the program internally coordinated?* Are provisions made for publicity, prayer support, arrangements, recruitment, etc.?
6. *Is there a failure line below which the program will be scrapped?* The establishment of a failure line could prevent many a program from becoming a hallowed tradition that cannot be dropped.
7. *Are there processes built into the program for effective follow-up after initial objectives have been met?*

Efficiency: This category seeks to measure whether we got where we wanted to get at the minimum cost to the total organization.

1. *Are the various kinds of record-keeping procedures necessary to undergird this program properly explained?*
2. *Do the resources of the congregation justify the use of the necessary time, talent, and treasure?* A small congregation will most likely be more limited in financial capability.
3. *Is it possible to develop, adapt, and improve various aspects of the program as the congregation works with it?* It must not be too rigid, yet the caution expressed above (Effectiveness, #2) must be remembered.
4. *Does the program try to be so efficient that it ends up doing too much too quickly, with the result that adequate training does not take place?* For example, sometimes there is not sufficient advance publicity and recruitment time.
5. *Are the people involved properly motivated to give their very best for the success of this program?*
6. *Does the congregation seek to match the spiritual gifts of its people to the tasks that must be carried out in this particular program?*
7. *Are those participating in the training program given enough to do on completion of their training to keep their interest alive, yet not so much as to kill their enthusiasm?*

It is readily admitted that not all of the questions in these four categories can be or need to be asked in each instance. However, most of the questions will be helpful for use in any evaluation that takes place, whether that evaluation occurs before the program is initiated, during its use, after its completion, or continuously.

In order to give the reader a sample evaluation based on the above questions, the evangelism program outlined in Kennedy's book, *Evangelism Explosion*, will be evaluated below. Most of the criticism of this program in Lutheran circles has come in the area of theology. The program has many great strengths, based on solid principles of training and equipping the saints. However, the mere success of a program does not guarantee that every method or theological emphasis is proper.

In the area of theology, questions two and three can be answered in the affirmative.

1. The motivation for evangelism in this program is not always the love of God in Jesus Christ. Kennedy writes that "the Church is a body under orders by Christ to share the gospel with the whole world."[8] While that is true, we would prefer to see the work of evangelism described

primarily as our loving response to God's gift of eternal life, as in 2 Corinthians 5:14.[9]

4. Actual sin is given a great deal of stress, but original sin, that innate corruption of each human being, is not stressed. The "Lemon Tree" and "Chinese Nature" illustrations of Chapter Six speak of this subject, and it would be wise to incorporate such an illustration in one's presentation of the Gospel.

5. An emphasis is placed on the work of the Holy Spirit in bringing about conversion, but sometimes Kennedy suggests that the Spirit brings us to the point of enabling us to decide for ourselves to receive Jesus Christ. Kennedy states, "God, the Holy Spirit, convicts us of our sins and calls us to receive Christ as our personal Savior."[10] God does not merely call us to receive Christ; He gives us that faith in Christ. Furthermore, the word "commitment," the heading of the third major section of the presentation, is better used in the sense of man's response to the Gospel after he has become a Christian. Otherwise, it conveys the idea that man is doing something to assist in his conversion.

On the positive side, Kennedy consistently uses the word "receive" instead of the less desirable "accept," as in the sentence, "Eternal life is received by trusting Jesus Christ."[11] The real concern is to distinguish between the theological work God does as the recreator and our psychological functioning, which includes the act of will described by the word "accept." As long as we understand that this act of will is totally the product of the Holy Spirit, even though we experience it as a psychological function, then we may use the word. Kennedy tries to steer away from the idea that man cooperates in arriving at his salvation, since he affirms that salvation is by grace through faith. One must recognize that it is difficult to be as theologically precise as one might like without becoming conversationally obscure, especially when talking with a non-Christian person.

6. Repentance is discussed in the presentation, but only in conjunction with the commitment section of the presentation.[12] It would be far better to talk about repentance when one talks about sin. Furthermore, when repentance is discussed, it is described as a willingness to turn from sin. That is not incorrect. However, it would be better to describe repentance as an acknowledgment of sins, genuine sorrow over sins, *and* the willingness to turn from them.

7. There is not enough stress in *Evangelism Explosion* on the use of God's Word and the sacraments as the means whereby the Christian is kept in the faith.

8. In one place the author writes, "We are saved by *trusting* in Jesus Christ, not by *saying* that we trust in Jesus Christ.[13] A consistent understanding of that statement would include a repudiation of prayer as a means whereby a person can come to faith. However, in another place prayer is listed as one of the five means of growth provided by God.[14] God both creates faith and sustains faith through His Word. Prayer is a response of faith; it does not create faith.

A good general piece of constructive criticism for this and most evangelism programs is that of Robert Schultz in a December, 1972, article in *The Cresset*. Schultz speaks of the value of presenting the Gospel not only in language that reflects Christ's work as our substitute, but also in language that reflects His work as conqueror of sin, death, and Satan.

In the area of objectives, questions two through five and number seven can be answered "yes." In response to question one, it must be said that the main emphasis of this program is to reach those who visit your church. In the second edition of *Evangelism Explosion*, Kennedy tries to broaden the application of the techniques of the book by including a chapter entitled "The Gospel for the Secular Mind." Certainly *Evangelism Explosion* can be used to reach more people than church visitors, but one must not assume that this program has all the techniques necessary to reach the Jehovah's Witness or to work cross-culturally.

In answer to question six, it can be said that specific, attainable, and measurable goals are not suggested or encouraged. Most evangelism programs do not suggest such goals, but it is wise to set goals, determine a time frame within which they will be met, decide on strategies to meet those goals, and regularly review progress towards those goals.

In the area of effectiveness, we answer "yes" to questions one, two, four, five, and seven. Question three is a question that probably will receive a "no" answer in most cases. Reevaluation is something that simply needs to be imposed on a program from without, if there is no provision from within.

Very few programs have a failure line below which the program will be scrapped. In most instances, ineffectiveness causes program leaders to make some changes and carry on, but lack of effectiveness might mean that the program should be stopped. Perhaps the reason why few programs have a failure line is that few programs have specific goals.

In the area of efficiency, the answers to the questions posed depend largely upon the energy and determination of the administrators of the program.

In summary, there are several theological points that most Lutherans would disagree with, at least as they are presented in the main textbook for this evangelism program. However, Kennedy rates high in the areas of objectives, effectiveness, and efficiency. With some changes in theological content, the Lutheran pastor could make excellent use of this program.

Chapter 2

The Correspondence Approach

There are other ways to reach the non-Christian with the Gospel besides home visitation. One of these is by mail. The number of strategies that can be utilized through this approach is limited; nevertheless, the mail has been used successfully. In some cases it may be the only way to reach certain people, such as reclusive apartment dwellers in urban and suburban areas.

There are companies that will send a mass mailing from a congregation to every resident living in a certain zip code or geographical area for a relatively small cost. Some congregations make use of this for public relations purposes or for invitations to special events. For those purposes, the use of such a mass mailing is pre-evangelism, but a congregation can also use this tool to share the Gospel message.

For example, if you use a local company to provide the names and addresses, The Gospel Publishing Association, P.O. Box 94368, Birmingham, Alabama 35215, can provide an eight-page tabloid for every home in your community under the name of your congregation, with two-and-a-half pages allowed to the congregation. You may also wish to contact Haines and Company by looking in your telephone directory. They publish a Reverse Telephone Directory that lists all the people by address. This would enable you to send a mailing to all people living on certain streets in your community.

Project Philip

Project Philip began at Holy Cross Lutheran Church, Moline, Illinois, as a result of Key 73, the interdenominational evangelism thrust of 1973 under the theme "Calling Our Continent to Christ." Bible correspondence materials and the suggestions for carrying out Project Philip came from the World Home Bible League.

In order to begin, the people of Holy Cross acquired a post office box and a mailing permit. They recruited a capable and dedicated person to be in charge of the mailing and filing. This person also became familiar with postal regulations in order to exercise good stewardship of money. Volunteers were recruited to stamp Bibles and study materials with the appropriate address and to deliver them to various places where people could pick them up. The name of Holy Cross never appeared on the materials, but people were asked to send their enrollment forms to "Bible Studies" at the post office box listed, Moline, Illinois.

There were three major ways in which Holy Cross enrolled people in the correspondence courses. First, they placed copies of the New Testament in the waiting rooms at local hospitals and area motels. An insert encouraged people to take the New Testaments as a gift and to enroll in a Bible correspondence course. Second, bulk mailings were sent out to the people of Moline as well as to the people of other communities. Third, advertisements were placed in local papers and shopper's guides. As a result, enrollments came not only from Moline, but from outside of Illinois and even outside of the United States.

One of the attractive features of Project Philip is that it does not require a great deal of training for the people who administer the program. This enables a number of people, who are by nature reticent to become involved, to participate in this program. They are easily able to prepare mailings, deliver New Testaments, file materials, correct returned courses, etc. In this way they can become involved in the work of the kingdom in a way that really matters, but in a way that does not expect more than they are able to do.

For these participants, as well as for the entire congregation, there are additional benefits. "This program broadens the outlook of the people," writes Pastor Eldor W. Haake, pastor of Holy Cross, "as to the vastness of the work the Lord has given us to do, to evangelize the world. It forces them to think beyond the limits of our congregation, and also beyond the limits of our own community." He writes further that there is now more involvement in Bible study at the church, as well as more involvement in the total ministry of the congregation.

While the purpose of the program can be to reach people for the church, this was not the purpose at Holy Cross. When people completed the correspondence course, they were encouraged to become affiliated with a Bible-teaching church. "How often this happens we have no way of knowing," states Pastor Haake. "However, many people did express their appreciation for this course and gave testimonies of personal, spiritual enrichment, and some informed us that they had very clearly learned the way to heaven." The people of Holy Cross did not identify their church in the printed invitations, and the promise was made in the enrollment materials that personal calls would not be made on them.

Prior to beginning Project Philip in your congregation, Pastor Haake recommends several things. "First of all, talk about it at great length with interested people, spending time in earnest prayer for the Lord's guidance and blessing. Then check with the local postmaster about a mailing permit and mailing rates for the lesson materials." One of the advantages of this program is the low cost. Only lesson materials and postage need to be budgeted, and bulk mailing rates keep the postage costs down. Thousands of people have been reached through Holy Cross for approximately $3.00 per person.

When these preparations have been made, "determine what materials you want to use for this correspondence course." Holy Cross Lutheran Church recommends the materials of the World Home Bible League. Finally, "determine your purpose, whether it is to increase the membership of your church, or whether it is to get the Word out to people in general who may be far away from your geographical area." Then get started, realizing that Project Philip requires a long-term commitment from a few key individuals and many other volunteers. Several hours each week are necessary to handle the correspondence, read through the returned lesson material, keep an up-to-date file, and send out the next course to those who have completed one of them.

Congregations that want to see their church grow as a result of Project Philip will want to identify their church in the New Testaments or Scripture portions, enrollment forms, mailings, and advertisements. Personal follow-up visits can be made on the people who respond, with further invitations given to worship services, the pastor's class, and the like. Some will not respond to the invitation to enroll in a correspondence course if they see that a particular church is identified. However, incorporation of a new Christian into the local body of Christ is much less likely to occur at the conclusion of a course if the congregation does not accept this responsibility.

Direct Mail Seminar

Any pastor and most laymen accumulate quite a stack of "junk mail" in a week's time. Such mail is annoying to some, but appreciated by others. One's appreciation for such mail is usually in inverse proportion to the amount that he receives. Nevertheless, direct mail solicitation works, or commercial enterprises would not be using it as extensively as they are.

In a six-hour Direct Mail Seminar, one can learn how to be equipped with the resources necessary to make use of direct mail. In this book we are specifically relating the Direct Mail Seminar to evangelism, although the seminar leader believes that direct mail can help a church in other areas of ministry as well.

Rev. Walter Mueller is the leader of the Specialized Ministries Center, 855 Welsh Rd., Maple Glen, Pennsylvania 19002, which conducts the Direct Mail Seminar. An ordained minister in the United Presbyterian Church, Mueller presents the material of the seminar in such a way as not to offend the religious sensibilities of the participants. His methods are theologically neutral.

After explaining the reasons behind the use of direct mail (after all, Paul's epistles were direct mail, says Mueller), the seminar leader shows how a church can get started in a direct mail program. He explains what is necessary in the areas of equipment, supplies, personnel, finances, and development of the mailing list.

Walter Mueller also shows how to prepare copy that gets results. Eye appeal and content are the two key factors, and good and bad examples of each are given, along with instructions on how to maximize the opportunities. One can easily see how a Direct Mail Seminar can have a good general effect on the total ministry of a given congregation, since the content of the seminar is broadly applicable.

The last four units of the seminar manual focus specifically on these four areas of ministry: communication, evangelism, education, and stewardship. For the purposes of this book, an explanation and evaluation of the chapter on evangelism follow.

The information provided in the unit on evangelism might better be called pre-evangelism, or what Mueller calls "indirect evangelism." He states in the Direct Mail Seminar manual that the seminar concentrates on indirect rather than direct evangelism, and he defines the purpose of indirect evangelism as follows: 'to whet the appetite' of the recipients so that they will come to church where they will hear the gospel and there be offered the opportunity to make a committment (sic) to Jesus Christ."[1]

Whether mailings are directed at the general public or at specific groups of people (such as newcomers to the community or visitors to your church), the Direct Mail Seminar will provide techniques for getting the best response from the letters that are sent. For example, a six- to eight-week, four-piece mail campaign prior to Easter Sunday is suggested for a time of the year when most Americans, whether churched or unchurched, are thinking about going to church. A good campaign at that time may bring many visitors who might not otherwise attend your church. Once they worship with you, the door is open for further contact with that family.

While the content of some of the sample letters provided in this unit is evangelistic, most of the emphasis is on welcoming people to the community, inviting them to your church, preparing them for a visit or telephone survey from a church member, or the like. This is why the section in the manual on evangelism is better called pre-evangelism. An individual church could indeed make its mailings evangelistic, but the purpose of the Direct Mail Seminar is to provide helps and techniques for getting the unchurched person to visit your church.

Libraries

Another way to make use of the U.S. mail is to provide various libraries in your community with free subscriptions to certain Christian magazines. The Jewish Chautauqua Society has for years put Jewish books into public libraries in order to help people understand Jews and Judaism. Why, then, can't Christians seek to place Christian literature in the same way and for similar purposes? Youth for Christ literature claims that their *Campus Life* magazine is in one-third of the high school libraries in America. They report a frequent librarians' complaint: "It's the magazine that disappears from our shelves most often." That is the kind of disappearing with which most Christians would have no problems! In addition, attempts are being made to distribute widely Campus Life books, which are aimed primarily at high school young people.

When we talk about libraries as evangelistic tools for the church, we mean the placement of books and magazines in public, high school, college, and university libraries. Such Christian literature can then be read by those who use these libraries and be an influence in their lives. One ought not overlook the use of a congregation's library, although that area does not actually fit into the correspondence approach.

Chapter 3

The Campus Approach

This chapter deals with that approach that speaks the word of the Gospel on the high school or college campus. Many of the parachurch organizations surveyed in this chapter carry out their ministry in other ways and places than on the campus, but their primary work is there. Some attention will be paid to those other types of ministries carried out by such parachurch organizations.

We will take a look at work in congregations, in parachurch organizations, and in bookstores.

Congregations

University Lutheran Chapel is a campus ministry, working among the 25,000 students of the University of Nebraska in Lincoln. Approximately 1,500 to 1,800 of these students are from LCMS congregations, so a solid core of Lutheran Christians enables the Chapel to reach out to Lutheran and non-Lutheran, Christian and non-Christian.

Rev. Jim Bauer has been pastor at the Chapel since 1978, and senior pastor since 1981. When the previous senior pastor retired in 1980, the Chapel needed to call an additional full-time worker. At that time two schools were developing their program of training lay evangelists for the congregations of the LCMS. Concordia College in St. Paul, Minnesota, and Christ College in Irvine, California, received exposure for this new approach to ministry at the Great Commission Convocation, held Nov. 6-9, 1980, in St. Louis. The Convocation and the needs of University Lutheran Chapel led to the call of Kent Stephens, a 1981 graduate of Christ College, as lay evangelist.

The ministry at Lincoln is a testimony to the success of the lay evangelist (Director of Evangelism) programs at Christ College and Concordia College. "The trained Lay Evangelist, or Director of Christian Outreach (as he has been named by us), is an exciting development in church ministry," states Pastor Bauer.

University Lutheran Chapel conducts an evangelistic ministry, based on the two track model. Track One evangelism involves various activities that are designed to attract students to the Chapel. For example, Friday evening is movie night, and many new faces show up in the crowd each week. On the weekend before classes began in the 1983-84 school year, a pig roast was held, and later on during the year, another college brought a dancing class to the facilities of the Chapel. A variety of other activities takes place regularly in order to promote the image of a vibrant, meaningful, and appealing Christian presence. These social events lay the groundwork for sharing the Gospel at a later time. The activities are extensively advertised in the daily college newspaper.

The distribution of nearly 2000 New Testaments has enhanced the outreach ministry. The Gospel appears in these New Testaments in outline form, and the customized covers point recipients to the Christian ministry of University Lutheran Chapel. These New Testaments were purchased from the World Home Bible League and financed by the offerings of Sunday school children throughout the Nebraska District.

Invitations to Sunday services and to mid-week Lenten services are another part of the Track One ministry. The Chapel regularly schedules an "Invite-a-Friend Sunday," thereby giving every student an opportunity to invite some friend. An evangelism team follows up on those individuals who visit. "Invite-a-Friend Sunday" is one factor that has led to a 40 percent increase in Sunday worship attendance over the past two years. Approximately 375 people worship at the Chapel each Sunday during the school year.

Over the past several years, the season of Lent has become a time of special outreach activity. The Chapel prints invitations to these mid-week services, asking students to distribute them to friends and classmates during evangelism visits and at other times. The services themselves feature a dramatic presentation in the place of the sermom and draw a large number of students.

Track Two evangelism includes two training cycles each year in Dialog Evangelism, known at the Chapel as "Reach-Out Evangelism." Depending upon the length of the semester, the training cycle lasts from 12 to 15 weeks. Trainees are involved in making calls with experienced trainers. Training sessions are held twice weekly in order to allow greater participation by Chapel members and in order to have more opportunities to find students in their dormitories, apartments, or homes. By the summer of 1983, 31 students had completed the Reach-Out training. Included in the training are study materials that address questions that commonly arise on the college campus, such as the validity and reliability of the Bible. Some on the college campus would suggest that one commits intellectual suicide by holding Christian beliefs, while others believe that the values of the Bible are dated.

Once each semester, lay evangelist Kent Stephens teaches a series of six classes on witnessing. In these classes, participants explore what the Bible has to say about witnessing and how they can develop a life-style of witnessing. Participants learn to take advantage of opportunities to witness in everyday situations with roommates, friends, and classmates. Basing part of his presentation on the testimony of the apostle Paul in the Book of Acts, Stephens teaches students how to share spontaneously what they believe and why.

Dialog Evangelism and witness training show how to present the truth claims of Christianity. There are a number of religious groups and cults on campus, so students need to learn their own beliefs well in order to measure the God-given truths of the Bible against the man-made teachings of various philosophies and religions.

Staff and students conduct a variety of weekly Bible studies at the Chapel and in the dormitories on various days of the week. These studies provide an opportunity to witness to one another and to friends who are invited to these meetings. About eight or nine such studies are conducted each semester, providing an opportunity for spiritual growth as well as evangelistic outreach. This facet of the ministry, the bread and butter of various Christian campus organizations, is also an important ingredient at University Lutheran Chapel.

Pastor Bauer teaches three adult classes each year, spring, summer, and fall. One young married couple has recently completed the classes and been confirmed. They were visited in the spring of 1983 by an evangelism team, and they heard the Gospel at that time. While they had not been attending church since their marriage, the birth of their first child had recently motivated them to consider a church home and some religious training for their child. As a result of the visit, the couple began attending the Chapel, enrolled in and completed the adult class, and became active members of the congregation. More than two dozen students have been confirmed over the past two years, and both Bauer and Stephens believe that the increasing effectiveness of their ministry will result in even more growth in the years to come.

"Evangelism is incorporated into the entire ministry from worship services to social events," says Stephens. "We are attempting to develop a sense of mission for every Chapel member." As a testimony to their success, each semester the worship attendance gradually increases as time goes on. Students draw other students as Sunday morning visitors and as guests at various social activities in increasing numbers.

Besides what has been done in congregations, much successful work has been accomplished by a number of *parachurch organizations*, to which we now turn our attention.

The Navigators

Taking their cue from the Great Commission (Matt. 28:18-20) and Christ's words about the scarcity of laborers (Matt. 9:37), The Navigators have as their aim "to multiply laborers in every nation and thus help fulfill Christ's Great Commission." Jack Mayhall, U.S. Director of The Navigators, writes further that in the United States the mission includes three major goals: to impact this country for Christ; to provide major resources for the global outreach of the organization; and to prepare trained laborers for other Christian ministries.[1]

More than any other organization surveyed on these pages, The Navigators combine evangelism with discipleship in a way that makes it difficult to distinguish between the two for the purposes of this book. This is commendable. Evangelism is not intended by our Lord to be one compartment of the Christian life, suitable for some Christians and unsuitable for others. Jesus intended all Christians to be witnesses (Acts 1:8), to be the salt of the earth (Matt. 5:13), and to be the light of the world (Matt. 5:14).

The Navigator ministry began with Dawson Trotman:

> In 1933, Dawson Trotman, founder of The Navigators, began teaching Navyman Les Spencer the principles of Christian growth. They spent many long hours together in Bible study, Scripture memorization and prayer. A shipmate of Spencer's soon asked him about the secret of his changed life. Spencer brought the new man to Trotman and said, "Teach him what you taught me!" Trotman's answer, "You teach him!" was the beginning of The Navigators.[2]

The Navigators follow the principle of spiritual reproduction, derived from the apostle Paul's words to Timothy, "And the things you have heard me say in the presence of many witnesses entrust to reliable men who will also be qualified to teach others." (2 Tim. 2:2 NIV) They seek to be used by God to win people to Christ. Then they teach the new converts the fundamentals of effective Christian living, until they are able to reproduce themselves spiritually and disciple others. Among these fundamentals are a devotional life, Bible study, memorization of Scripture, prayer, meditation on Scripture, personal witness, and testimony.

According to the 1981 annual report, there are over 1,900 full-time staff at work in more than 38 countries. Navigator ministries are under the direction of national leaders in 12 of these countries. In the United States, American Navigators are involved in disciple-making ministries in every state and on 140 campuses, 107 military bases, and 85 communities. These figures demonstrate the primary emphasis of the ministry of The Navigators to be on the campus.

The U.S. headquarters office is located at Glen Eyrie in Colorado Springs, Colorado. It provides administrative support for the American staff, the publication of ministry materials, and centralized development and communications services for Navigators worldwide. The address is The Navigators, P.O. Box 6000, Colorado Springs, Colorado 80934.

Many conferences are held each year in the picturesque setting of Glen Eyrie, focusing on discipleship in the local church. A 320-acre camp for young people and adults is located in nearby Pike National Forest. Eagle Lake Camp has been a part of the Navigator ministry since 1953.

In recognition of the fact that many countries in the world today are closed to missionaries, The Navigators have developed a program known as Missionary Associates. This program helps teams of professional men and women, experienced in disciple-making, to secure vocational positions in these countries. There are 60 missionary associates ministering in 21 countries as teachers, nurses, doctors, engineers, scientists, and the like.

The current NavPress catalog lists three tools for evangelism. One of these is an evangelistic tract; the other two demonstrate the above-mentioned marriage between evangelism and discipleship. One of these two is called "Leader's Guide for Evangelistic Bible Studies," showing how to conduct an evangelistic Bible study based on the Gospel of John. The other tool is an actual Bible study, geared especially for the non-Christian and requiring no advance preparation, except by the leader. This type of Bible study is the major tool for Navigator use on campus.

Actually there are many other evangelism tools used by The Navigators, although they are not listed in the catalog as such. One of the most popular discipleship tools, called "The 2:7 Series," contains some training for witness and a great deal of training which raises the level of the spiritual life of the individual Christian, so that he becomes better equipped and more motivated to witness. Based on Col. 2:7, "Rooted and built up in Him, strengthened in the faith as you were taught, and overflowing with thankfulness" (NIV), this series is designed to build up Christians in Christ and teach them to live a consistent Christian life. At first glance, "The 2:7 Series" appears to be a tool for the purpose of Christian education, but a more thorough look yields a disciple-making course that has as one of its goals to lead others to know and trust in Jesus Christ as Savior. Indeed, all Christian education should have this as one of its major goals.

Other listings in the catalog further demonstrate the Navigator interest in the spiritual birth of the Christian. For example, Leroy Eims has written *The Lost Art of Disciple Making*, and Jim Petersen is the author of *Evangelism As a Lifestyle*. The reader would do well to compare the youth and adult instructional materials of his denomination with Navigator materials in order to help answer the vexing question about backdoor losses.

The bi-monthly magazine of The Navigators, *Discipleship Journal*, has some of the same results in people's lives as "The 2:7 Series," although not with the same concentrated, goal-oriented purposes. It has reached a subscription level of 35,000 in the short time since its inception in January, 1981.

The Navigators also have a cassette tape ministry, including many tapes on the twin subjects of discipleship and evangelism. Dozens of messages on other subjects are also available, but several titles in the evangelism section catch one's eye: "Vision for Evangelism," "Friendship Evangelism," and "The Art of Personal Friendship," the last tape by Mr. Lorne Sanny, President of The Navigators since 1956.

In summary, one-on-one contacts with non-Christians are emphasized by The Navigators; small group Bible studies are a next step after the friendship of the individual has been won, whether the Navigator is working on the college campus, in the military, or in a community; and undergirding all of this is an emphasis upon the spiritual life of the witness. The perceptive reader will notice some of the same theological traits that were criticized in the evaluation of *Evangelism Explosion* in the first chapter, but such differences of theological orientation do not disqualify Navigator materials from being used by a wide variety of denominations.

Inter-Varsity Christian Fellowship

Among the four organizations in this chapter that evangelize primarily on the college campus, Inter-Varsity Christian Fellowship (IVCF or IV) has the earliest roots, although the first U.S. chapter was begun at the University of Michigan in 1939, some years after the beginning of The Navigators. IVCF has its roots in a student movement in England, which began in the 1870s. Years later the movement spread to Canada and the United States. Since 1939, IVCF has expanded to include more than 32,000 students and over 335 trained staff on 825 college and university campuses. The President of IVCF is John W. Alexander, and the headquarters are located at 233 Langdon, Madison, Wisconsin 53703, on the campus of the University of Wisconsin.

IVCF's statement of purpose is as follows:

> The *purpose* of the Inter-Varsity Christian Fellowship is to establish, assist and encourage at colleges, universities, nursing schools and other comparable educational institutions in the United States of America *groups of students* (and faculty members) who *witness to the Lord Jesus Christ as God incarnate* and have these major objectives:
>
> 1. Evangelism: To lead others to personal faith in Christ as Lord and Savior.
>
> 2. Discipleship: To help Christians grow toward maturity as disciples of Christ, by study of the Bible, by prayer and by Christian fellowship.
>
> 3. Missions: To present the call of God to the world mission of the Church; to help students and faculty to discover God's role for them.[3]

Inter-Varsity works with four major groups of people in its ministry: students, faculty, community friends, and staff. Community friends are those alumni, pastors, business people, and others who encourage and assist in campus visitation, prayer meetings, and the raising of financial support for staff members.

IVCF serves students and faculty by providing literature to help them accomplish the three objectives of the organization. Emphasis is placed upon developing spiritual leaders among Christian students rather than depending upon staff for all the necessary programming. *Student Leadership Handbook* and *Faculty Handbook* are two of the basic tools produced by Inter-Varsity. Inter-Varsity Press has various publications helpful to the Christian student, among them writings of John R. W. Stott and J. I. Packer, two well-known authors in the evangelical world. For example, *Campus & Church* by John W. Alexander and *Basic Christianity* by John Stott are resources for campus evangelism. IV has published *Out of the Saltshaker*, by Rebecca Manley Pippert, a book dealing with evangelism as a way of life. Will Metzger's *Tell the Truth* deals with the subject of witnessing, and Paul Little's *How To Give Away Your Faith* has become a classic on the same subject. The award-winning *HIS* magazine helps the student relate his faith to the challenge of secularism, humanism, and the other "isms" he faces on campus.

Special training programs, weekend conferences, missions conventions, summer camps, and a variety of other programs assist in the total ministry of Inter-Varsity. Cedar Campus is a camp facility owned by IVCF near Cedarville, Michigan, that serves as the major camping resource.

Like other Christian campus ministries, the small group Bible study is one of the key methods of IV. Students in small groups develop friends who truly care about them, and, in some instances, they come to trust in Christ as their Savior through the study of the Bible in these groups. Some of the more than 2,000 college students who became Christians in 1980 through the witness of Inter-Varsity were greatly affected in the small group Bible study.

Special evangelism training for students is supplemented by a number of evangelism projects, such as the Port Aransas (TX) Evangelism Project. Twenty-five students and staff visited this fishing town near Corpus Christi during the spring break in 1980, spending afternoons on the beach in pairs and three, witnessing to students. Similar projects occur annually at Fort Lauderdale, Florida, and Mackinac Island, Michigan, during the spring or summer. Twentyone-hundred Productions is the special film branch of IVCF.

Training and motivation in the area of missions is another aspect of Inter-Varsity's evangelistic goals, but on a world-wide scale. The Urbana conferences are the most significant and largest student missions conventions in America. In 1981 there were 17,000 students, hundreds of experienced missionaries, and many top-notch speakers and workshops that gathered together on the campus of the University of Illinois in Urbana for a gathering hailed by many mission boards and denominational leaders as the major recruiting force for both foreign and domestic missions.

Through Student Training in Missions (STIM), 171 students spent the summer of 1981 scattered in 40 different countries working in a cross-cultural missionary situation. An Overseas Training Camp with IV can give a prospective missionary an opportunity to find out what it is like to live in another country before he commits himself to such a career.

In addition to its ministry at colleges and universities, Inter-Varsity offers specialized ministries through its Nurses Christian Fellowship (NCF), Student Foreign Missions Fellowship (SFMF), and Theological Students Fellowship (TSF). NCF assists nursing students in helping people face crises, as they bring a spiritual, physical and emotional perspective from a Christian vantage point. SFMF is organized on many Christian college campuses to add impetus to the cause of missions. TSF encourages academic excellence among future pastors and theologians with a commitment to the full authority and relevance of Scripture. It publishes the international journal *Themelios* three times a year.

The doctrinal basis of IVCF will not cause any problems for a confessional Lutheran, except that it is so briefly stated. Some of the teachings that underlie these brief statements would evoke some disagreement. Five points comprise the Inter-Varsity doctrinal position:
1. The unique divine inspiration, entire trustworthiness and authority of the Bible.
2. The deity of our Lord Jesus Christ.
3. The necessity and efficacy of the substitutionary death of Jesus Christ for the redemption of the world, and the historic fact of His bodily resurrection.
4. The presence and power of the Holy Spirit in the work of regeneration.
5. The expectation of the personal return of our Lord Jesus Christ.[4]

Much more could be said about Inter-Varsity Christian Fellowship. It requires its staff to be active in a local congregation. It provides training helps in witness and evangelism that reflect the influence of D. James Kennedy. It tends to look upon prayer in evangelism as a means of grace. It has a strong emphasis upon the training of the individual Christian. It identifies with the definition of evangelism from the Lausanne Covenant (Clause 4):

4. *The Nature of Evangelism*

To evangelize is to spread the good news that Jesus Christ died for our sins and was raised from the dead according to the Scriptures, and that as the reigning Lord he now offers the forgiveness of sins and the liberating gift of the Spirit to all who repent and believe. Our Christian presence in the world is indispensable to evangelism, and so is that kind of dialogue whose purpose is to listen sensitively in order to understand. But evangelism itself is the proclamation of the historical, biblical Christ as Savior and Lord, with a view to persuading people to come to him personally and so be reconciled to God. In issuing the Gospel invitation we have no liberty to conceal the cost of discipleship. Jesus still calls all who would follow him to deny themselves, take up their cross, and identify themselves with his new community. The results of evangelism include obedience to Christ, incorporation into his church and responsible service in the world.

(1 Cor. 15:3, 4; Acts 2:32-39; John 20:21; 1 Cor. 1:23; 2 Cor. 4:5; 5:11, 20; Luke 14:25-33; Mark 8:34; Acts 2:40, 47; Mark 10:43-45)[5]

Suffice it to say that IVCF does an admirable job of attaining its three objectives of evangelism, discipleship, and missions.

Campus Crusade for Christ

Campus Crusade was started in 1951 on the campus of U.C.L.A. by Bill and Vonette Bright. For the past 30 years the objective of the organization has remained the same: to reach people with the Good News of God's love and forgiveness and to build them in their faith so that they may win and disciple others. The Great Commission is embedded in every aspect of the Campus Crusade ministry.

Bill Bright began work on the college campus because he believed it to be one of the greatest sources of manpower and planning from which to reach out to the rest of the world. Since the early days, Campus Crusade has branched out into many other areas of ministry, but "the heart of the U.S. ministry is still the college campus."[6] In the U.S. 57 percent of the Campus Crusade field staff was involved in college ministry during 1981. Another seven percent of the field staff was involved in ministry on high school campuses.

The strength of the campus ministry is the small group Bible study. Students who show an interest are invited to join such a group. The group leader makes a fourfold commitment to that new participant: to spend time with the student, to show him how to witness, to train him to lead a Bible study, and eventually to encourage him to lead a discipleship group of his own. In this way the campus ministry multiplies itself.

Many other special ministries assist the basic campus ministry. Musical groups, traveling speakers (such as the well-known author and speaker Josh McDowell), and drama troupes travel around the United States. Campus Crusade publishes an evangelistic newspaper in two editions for both high school and college audiences. This paper, called *Live Option*, presents the relevance of a relationship with Jesus Christ.

The Athletes in Action (AIA) teams compete against top college, university, and national teams throughout the world. Team members present the Gospel to spectators during halftimes and in small group meetings with the other team. While the basketball team of Athletes in Action is most well known, AIA also competes in gymnastics, track, wrestling, volleyball, soccer, and softball. AIA staff help organize Bible studies for professional athletes in baseball, football, tennis, golf, and hockey. *Athletes in Action* is a quarterly magazine that relates the Christian faith to the world of sports.

The Atlanta-based Executive Ministry reaches out to top-level businessmen and women through evangelistic dinner parties hosted by prominent Christian couples in the community. The Family Ministry offers conferences and tape packages to help enrich marriage, offer assistance in parent-child relationships, and prepare people for marriage. The Christian Living Seminar lays the foundation for a successful Christian life and teaches skills in the area of personal evangelism. The Military Ministry works with military personnel and their families. "P.S." (Prison) Ministries works with prison chaplains, helping to conduct institutional chapel programs and to plan strategies of discipleship and evangelism for inmates, parolees, and probationers. Christian Embassy staff members work among government officials and the diplomatic community in Washington, D.C., and the United Nations. The entire ministry of Campus Crusade is supported by a strong prayer ministry, including a 24-hour Prayer/Care telephone service, a ministry in which Mrs. Vonette Bright has a personal involvement.

At its headquarters in Arrowhead Springs (mailing address: Campus Crusade for Christ International, Arrowhead Springs, San Bernardino, California 92414), Campus Crusade has established its International School of Theology. This school provides training for men and women on a seminary level, offering the master of arts, master of divinity, and doctor of ministry degrees. Two extension schools in Kenya and the Philippines were opened in 1981.

The publishing arm of Campus Crusade is known as Here's Life Publishers, P.O. Box 1576, San Bernardino, California 92402. They publish the books, Bible studies, and training resources that are produced within the organization.

The aspect of Campus Crusade's ministry that has received the most attention in recent years is the Here's Life campaign, which seeks to serve as an evangelistic arm of the local church in bringing people to Christ and the church. Local Christians are trained in prayer, personal evangelism, discipleship, and "I found it!" media campaigns. The "Jesus" film, a two-hour documentary on the life of Christ according to the Gospel of Luke, is one of the tools developed to assist Here's Life, particularly in areas where there are few or no local Christians. Steps are being taken to translate the film into the 163 languages that are spoken by at least one million people in the world, with the result that 95 percent of the world's population could see and understand the film. In some places where the communication of the Gospel is limited, the "Jesus" film, radio broadcasts, and direct mail will be used as extensively as possible.

Some Christians have questions about theology and methodology, as practiced in the Here's Life campaign. As one pastor whose congregation participated in "Here's Life, St. Louis," this author must question the telephone shotgun approach, where callers invited the people of the community to make a profession of faith in Jesus Christ over the phone. This kind of impersonal contact, preceded only by a media campaign, produced a certain number of "decisions." However, when the follow-up booklets were delivered, we discovered in each instance that people responded only out of curiosity or had simply given an insincere verbal response. In church after church, no real conversions occurred and no new persons joined the church. It is undoubtedly true that some people were reached for Christ by the campaign workers, but most of these were those who were already Christian or whose contacts with God's Word and other Christians had brought them to the threshold of faith, a threshold that would have been crossed soon anyway.

Dr. Win Arn, president and executive director of the Institute for American Church Growth (Suite 150, 709 East Colorado, Pasadena, California 91101), has published an incisive critique of "Here's Life, America" in an article first appearing in the magazine *Church Growth: America* and was later reprinted in *The Pastor's Church Growth Handbook*. In it he has both positive and negative things to say about "Here's Life, America."

Among Arn's positive comments are these: "Campus Crusade is doing something." Criticism from those not involved in evangelistic work has a hollow sound to it; armchair evangelists are a dime a dozen. "It is their best effort to date. . . .a creative new way to touch people." "Evangelism has moved closer to the local church." "Lay people are being trained and involved." "High visibility is being achieved."[7]

Dr. Arn also has some criticisms. First, he questions the major goal of "Here's Life." Success ought not to be measured by the number of "decisions" that are made, but by the number of people who become disciples of Christ as a result of the work. Second, he doubts whether "Here's Life" is effective evangelism. Most participating congregations had the same response that the author's congregation had. After taking some sample surveys in both Indianapolis and Fresno, Arn discovered that among the 400 churches surveyed, only 3.3 percent of every 100 "decisions" became active members of any church and that 42 percent of these came into the church by transfer. Third, Arn claims that the emphasis upon follow-up was insufficient and the subject of incorporation into the church hardly mentioned. Arn's critique suggests that Christian churches ought to spend their time, energy, and finances in more productive kinds of evangelistic programming.[8]

At the risk of repeating an evaluation that is all too familiar in some circles, a few things need to be said about the "Four Spiritual Laws" booklet, which is the basic witnessing tool used in Campus Crusade programs.

The use of the word "law" in the title of a booklet for presenting the Gospel is confusing at best and poor theology at worst. The thought expressed on page 10, that "You can receive Christ right now by faith through prayer" implies that it is the prayer of the individual that makes one a Christian. It is certainly possible that upon occasion a person becomes a Christian during such a prayer, but one ought not to give the impression that prayer is a means by which God creates faith in a person. That happens only through God's Word and Sacrament. Furthermore, the problem of "decision" theology is most evident in this tract, where the author does not acknowledge that faith is a gift of God, and not the result of the work or decision of man. "For it is by grace you have been saved, through faith— and this not from yourselves, it is the gift of God—not by works, so that no one can boast" (Eph. 2:8, 9 NIV). We are not saved "by faith through prayer," but by grace through faith.

In spite of some sincere and serious criticism of certain aspects of the work of Campus Crusade, the Christian rejoices in the fact that ministry is being carried out in the name of Jesus Christ and that people are coming to faith in Him, growing in that faith, and reproducing themselves as a result of the ministry of Campus Crusade for Christ.

Fellowship of Christian Athletes

"The star of athletic influence is shining brightly now. It may not always be so, but it is now. And I believe the Fellowship of Christian Athletes is the most effective group in America for passing along the influence of Christianity." So says Tom Landry, head coach of the Dallas Cowboys. Billy Graham has said of the Fellowship of Christian Athletes (FCA), "It's one of the most effective movements in this nation for the presentation of the Gospel to young people."[9]

The beginnings of FCA can be traced back to 1947, when Oklahoma student coach Don McClanen gave a talk on "Making My Vocation Christian" and began forming an idea that gathered momentum over the next seven years. On November 12, 1954, the bylaws of FCA were adopted, and the organization was born. In 1955, baseball immortal Branch Rickey, after whom the local St. Louis chapter is named, and Pittsburgh businessmen underwrote a year's budget. The next year Don McClanen became the first president of the organization. The national headquarters were established in Kansas City, where they are located today at 8701 Leeds Rd., Kansas City, Missouri 64129.

The purpose of FCA is "to present to athletes and coaches, and all whom they influence, the challenge and adventure of receiving Jesus Christ as Savior and Lord, serving Him in their relationships and in the fellowship of the church."[10]

The ministry of FCA focuses on six main areas, the first two of which are its most significant ministries: (1) junior and senior high huddles; (2) college fellowships; (3) adult chapters; (4) national conferences; (5) coaches activities; and (6) church involvement. The activities and purposes of huddles and fellowships are not specifically evangelistic, although the environment exists in which athletes may come to trust in Jesus Christ as their Savior. Emphasis is upon Bible study and discussion, with guest speakers, tapes, films and other options available for meetings. FCA works among both men and women.

Some local FCA chapters have a speakers' bureau with a dual purpose: to tell the story of FCA and so witness for Christ, and to raise money to support the local FCA program. Professional athletes volunteer their services during the off-season, making themselves available as banquet speakers, or to speak at small group meetings, special services, and the like. Their honorarium is returned to the organization for the support of FCA.

The official publication of the Fellowship of Christian Athletes is *The Christian Athlete*, a 32-page tabloid that seeks to relate the Christian faith to the life of athletic competition. The national newspaper of FCA is *The Widening Circle*, which tells the story of FCA's ministry.

Cassette tapes are available for purchase with optional discussion questions. Featured on these tapes are such sports personalities as Tom Landry, Roger Staubach, and Madeline Manning Jackson. Films and filmstrips complement the ministry, spotlighting such people as former major league baseball player Jerry Kindall, soccer player Kyle Rote, Jr., and former NFL star Tim Foley.

A 29-member national board of directors runs the organization with total responsibility for the FCA program in the United States. State and regional organizations usually have a board of directors and a voluntary or salaried chairman. They seek to carry out on a state or regional level what the national organization is trying to do on a national scale. Local adult chapters are the backbone of the Fellowship of Christian Athletes in most areas. Adult members meet regularly, give of their time to support the high school and college programs, and support the organization financially.

The FCA is an interdenominational organization, which stresses that local FCA groups should have a good working relationship with the institutional church. While there is much to be said for those doctrines that most Christians have in common, the nature of an interdenominational organization suggests that one should avoid that false kind of ecumenism in this or any such organization, an ecumenism which blurs the differences of belief between various church bodies and suggests that we all believe the same thing.

Today there is strong Roman Catholic participation in the FCA movement. Former Dallas quarterback Roger Staubach, pro football Hall of Famer Alan Ameche, and NBA center Kent Benson are active Catholics and FCA members. Notre Dame and Holy Cross boast energetic FCA fellowships.

Tom Landry is right. The star of athletic influence is shining brightly now. Christians would do well to take advantage of opportunities to reach young men and women for Christ in a way that might reach some who would otherwise never be reached.

Young Life

Young Life is the first of two organizations covered in these pages that work primarily on the high school campus, while those that have preceded Young Life in this chapter work primarily on the college campus.

In order to get a firsthand glimpse of Young Life, join me as we visit a Young Life meeting at the home of a teenager in Connecticut. When his mother was asked to host the next weekly Young Life club meeting, she was not anticipating the 60 laughing, talking youngsters that descended upon her home.

The size of the living room and the number of youth forced them to exchange that meeting place for the front lawn. At 7:30 a young fellow in bluejeans began strumming his guitar, and the next 30 minutes were filled with contemporary spiritual songs and some popular rock.

> At about eight o'clock the singing ended. Most of the youngsters sat down on the grass, cross-legged, looking up at the leader who had taken the top porch step as a rostrum. Like the boys, he wore jeans and an open-collared sports shirt. Until now he had been merely another member of the crowd, drifting here and there, chatting with anyone who cared to talk . . . .
>
> Now, from the top step, he launched into a brief talk. It took scarcely 10 minutes and it was based on a Biblical theme in contemporary terms. What he said could not be characterized as a sermon. It

was too colloquial, an easy conversation with friends. The manner in which he stressed the wisdom of the Bible's message sounded so practical, so rational, that any other attitude toward life seemed absurd. He spoke of trust: people trusting their friends, people trusting their parents, people trusting Jesus Christ . . . .

By eight-thirty the meeting ended. The young people left as they had come, in cars, on bicycles, on motorbikes, on foot, and Elm Avenue was quiet again.[11] (Reprinted with permission from The Saturday Evening Post Company, 1975.)

The organization which began this Connecticut club and hundreds of others like it had its beginnings in the late 1930s in Texas. A seminary student at Dallas Theological Seminary was asked by the minister of a suburban church to try to reach young people for Jesus Christ. James Rayburn started seeking out the kids where they were. He went to athletic contests and school events. He talked with them over pizza and Coke. He showed a genuine interest in knowing them and their needs. He established friendships with these high school youth and then sought to introduce them to Jesus Christ and show how Christ could meet their needs.

Young Life meetings began in 1938. The ministry caught on and expanded to such an extent that Young Life was incorporated in 1941. In the early 1940s, camp ministry became an important part of Young Life, and it remains so today.

Rayburn was succeeded as president of the organization in 1964 by Bill Starr. Starr is best known for introducing and implementing the team concept of leadership at Young Life. During his tenure, the education and training of leaders at all levels was strengthened and expanded. In 1967 the current president, Bob Mitchell, took office. Although its first leader was an ordained Presbyterian minister, Young Life describes itself as non-denominational. Contact with Young Life bears that out.

Today there are over 1,100 Young Life clubs in the United States and 10 foreign countries. There is a weekly attendance of more than 70,000 young people. Young Life is staffed by 600 full-time and 200 part-time personnel and assisted by 6,000 volunteers. *Young Life* magazine is the main organ of communication regarding Young Life programs, activities, and purposes.

Young Life owns and operates seven major camp properties in British Columbia, California, Colorado, Minnesota, New York, and North Carolina. Each summer about 17,000 campers spend a week at one of these resorts, while weekend camps attract 50,000 children during the school year. Camp programs provide young people excitement and adventure in a Christian atmosphere.

Young Life has established homes where some of the 10,000 youngsters, who run away from home each week, can find refuge. Young Life leaders seek to minister to some of these teenagers from their Christian perspective and persuade them to return to their homes. Young Life is actively involved in all of the problems of young people in approximately 300 communities in North America. The outreach extends to urban, suburban, and small city areas. Their ministry has been sufficiently impressive to attract the attention and support of Senator Mark Hatfield, who has served on the Young Life board and whose wife is presently a board member.

The story of Young Life is told by Char Meredith in the book *It's a Sin to Bore a Kid* (Word Books). The address of the organization is Young Life International Service Center, 720 Monument St., P. O. Box 520, Colorado Springs, Colorado 80901.

"Young Life's purpose is to introduce adolescents to Jesus Christ and His relevance to life today. We strive to communicate these concepts in simple, understandable terms and through meaningful friendships with high school people."[12] Recent changes in the organization have led it to begin working among junior high school students as well. Young Life does an excellent job of accomplishing its purpose.

Youth for Christ

What do Ray Stedman, Johnny Cash, astronaut Major Jack Lousma, Ted Engstrom, Billy Graham, and Cliff Barrows all have in common? They have all, at one time or another, been actively involved in the programs and activities of Youth for Christ (YFC). Few people know that Billy Graham first received national attention when he became the first full-time staff person for Youth for Christ in 1945. It was during the years after World War II that evangelist Cliff Barrows became song leader on the Billy Graham team. Ted Engstrom was the third president of Youth for Christ, while Jack Lousma credits YFC with his involvement as a leader in his church's youth program. Johnny Cash and Ray Stedman have both served on the board of trustees of the organization.

About the time that Young Life was getting organized in the 1930s, YFC was taking shape. It was their goal to reach the high school youth of our nation and the world for Jesus Christ. In the early 1940s the movement gained momentum. In 1943 the first rally was held under the name of "Youth for Christ." From that point on the movement grew rapidly until the founding convention of YFC was convened on July 22, 1945, in

Winona Lake, Indiana. At that convention, Torrey Johnson, a Chicago pastor, was elected as the first president of the organization, and a seven-point doctrinal platform was adopted. This platform still stands today and affirms basic evangelical truths: an infallible Scripture, the Triune God, the deity of Jesus Christ and His vicarious death, the need of salvation for lost mankind, the power of the Holy Spirit, the coming resurrection, and the spiritual unity of believers in Christ. No Christian with a firm faith in Christ and confidence in His Word would have any difficulty with this statement, at least as far as it goes. The difficulty would arise when some of the points are expanded.

The movement spread rapidly through America and the world. In 1948, YFC sponsored the first Congress on World Evangelism[13] in Beatenburg, Switzerland. More such world congresses were held in various cities throughout the world over the next 15 years.

In the United States, Jack Hamilton came to the international office in order to develop the program of YFC on a national scale. Bible clubs began in the high schools in the 1950s. Bible quizzing, talent contests, and other imaginative ministries were also begun. In 1951, the Youth Guidance program (originally known as Lifeline) was developed under the leadership of Gordon McLean for the purpose of reaching troubled youth, developing their self-image, and communicating basic Christian values as the foundation of growth for the whole person.

It was under the leadership of YFC's second president, Dr. Bob Cook, that the decision was made to specialize on the teenage population. Subsequent presidents, Ted Engstrom, Carl "Kelly" Bihl, and Dr. Sam Wolgemuth, continued the work and constantly refined the methods and means of reaching teenagers for Jesus Christ. More details on the history of Youth for Christ can be read in James Hefley's book about the organization, *God Goes to High School* (Word Books).

Under the leadership of current president Dr. Jay Kesler, Youth for Christ works with churches to reach out to teenagers and their families through five basic ministries: Campus Life clubs, youth guidance, family concern, literature, and media.

Campus Life clubs hold informal evening meetings every other week for high school students. The meetings last approximately one hour and include games, skits, and an open discussion of some issue of interest to teens—loneliness, drugs, peer pressure, vocation, and the like. A Campus Life staff member wraps up the evening with a summary that relates the evening's discussion to Christian principles. Over 1,700 high schools in America have Campus Life clubs, led by adults trained for such work. Beyond the regular meetings, staff members spend time at school events and contact young people wherever they are and consequently spend much time in personal counseling.

Dr. J. Allan Petersen, nationally known specialist in marriage and family life, is the founder and director of Family Concern. Family Affair Seminar is a Biblically based weekend experience, dedicated to strengthening the marriage and family life by means of lectures and personal group assignments. The seminar is brought to an area by the sponsorship of a local church or group of churches; it is led either by Dr. Petersen or Bruce Narramore.

The literature ministry of YFC includes *Campus Life* magazine, which recently merged organizationally with *Christianity Today*, Campus Life books, *The Way* and *Reach Out* (youth editions of *The Living Bible* and *The Living New Testament*), and the Campus Life Leader's Guide, which enables youth leaders to adapt *Campus Life* magazine for use in youth meetings. *Campus Life* magazine has an estimated readership of one million, with circulation at approximately one-fourth that amount.

The media ministry of YFC includes television and radio programs, such as the "Johnny Cash Youth Special" and "Is There a Family in the House?". "Family Forum" is a daily radio program featuring Dr. Jay Kesler answering questions about family problems directed to him by listeners.

Over 1,100 full-time and 3,800 part-time staff and volunteers work in the United States, while hundreds more work in some 62 countries around the world. Overseas, the YFC philosophy is to establish an indigenous ministry in every country in which they have a program. A comparison of figures shows YFC to be slightly larger than its older cousin, Young Life.

In its Campus Life Operations Manual, Youth for Christ spells out its understanding of evangelism, rejecting both the buttonholing style of evangelism and the present style of "evangelism" that fails to speak the Gospel. Disciple-making is a large part of YFC's understanding of evangelism, for when a Campus Life club comes to a high school campus, it comes there for the long term. The focus is not on getting decisions, but on developing relationships with kids, speaking the Gospel to them in a way that shows how the Gospel fills their deepest needs, and following through in order that the fruit of the Gospel may remain (John 15:16).

Youth for Christ believes that high school ministry is crucial and strategic. It is the last chance to touch a total cross section of the community, because once graduation is over a generation splits forever. At the same time, high school is a time in life where for the first time young people have reached a level of maturity. While some might challenge the validity of the last assertion, it is undoubtedly true that the high school years can be the turning point in many a young person's life. It is also true that the high school is a strategic place for ministry. As the Operations Manual says it, "The high school is actually the funnel of the community; nearly everybody goes through it." That certain Christian organizations are engaged in ministry to the high school student should give every believer cause to give thanks to God.

Bookstores

Another way for Christians to reach the young people on campus is by arranging for the sale of certain Christian books in the college and high school bookstores. If the right kind of books are made available, there will be times when a young person, who is searching for answers, will pick up a book and read it. The same can be said for public bookstores and even church libraries and bookstores.

Chapter 4

The Educational Approach

The evangelism approaches surveyed in this chapter involve the presentation of the Gospel either at the church through one of its educational agencies or in the home of one of the church members. There are several exceptions to this guideline, which illustrate the difficulty of placing evangelism programs into categories. Excluded from this chapter are those programs that occur when the congregation or a number of congregations assemble as a large group. They will be surveyed in the final chapter. The programs in this chapter are those that utilize the small group or the classroom. The chapter deals with the educational approach first among children and then among adults.

Vacation Bible School

First Lutheran Church, Windsor, Ontario, is a downtown congregation, which, in 1975, had 700 communicant members, but a Sunday School of only 45, including teachers. There were very few children and young couples at worship services, and the congregation seemed very much turned in on itself. That same year the congregation initiated a bus ministry to strengthen the Sunday School and had its first Vacation Bible School (VBS). Today the Sunday School has 220 regular attenders, about half of them from non-Lutheran homes, with 90 children brought each Sunday on two buses. The energy directed toward the Sunday School has complemented the work put into VBS and vice versa.

That first VBS had an enrollment of 97, not a remarkable figure for a congregation that size, and a distant figure from the 390 that attended in 1982.

"First we switched our time to the evenings, from 6:15 p.m. to 9:15 p.m.," says Pastor Matthias Krey. "This meant more workers and greater participation from the adults. We selected the first two weeks of July, because that is about a week or two after school lets out here in Canada and it is before families leave on their vacations." The evening time makes the family car more accessible. It enables parents to have several summer evenings free, while the children are at VBS. More members are available for serving on the VBS staff in a day when working mothers are the norm. The evening hours are not a hindrance for most of the pre-school children, who can sleep late the next day.

The staff of 90 is comprised primarily of the Sunday School staff, but a Sunday School staff of 38 obviously needs much help from other members of First Lutheran. The recruitment of staff is no problem. As a matter of fact, some workers want to know why they have not been called on again to teach in a given year. That is the result of the VBS policy of seeking to involve 10 percent new staff each year. This means that First Lutheran now has a reservoir of well-trained and experienced teachers and helpers.

"Our teachers are held in high esteem," comments Pastor Krey, "and they themselves know that they hold a position of importance." The teachers are installed during a church service prior to VBS, and, after VBS, they receive recognition certificates at yet another service. They are individually recognized, receiving the thanks of the pastor, church officers, and the entire congregation.

Preparation for class time takes place in various ways. The pastor leads the teachers and helpers through the materials that are to be taught. A committee of the congregation selects its own crafts. All year long, members have their eyes open for beautiful, meaningful, and easily made projects. About 30 adults prepare samples of the crafts to be used and introduce them to the teachers and helpers at a special meeting prior to the VBS.

Publicity begins about six weeks before VBS. In addition to the announcements made to the congregation, the message of VBS spreads by word of mouth. Some 3,000 flyers are distributed to people in the community. The members of First Lutheran stand at the entrance of the public schools, handing out flyers as school is let out.

However, one of the most important parts of First Lutheran's publicity has taken place years in advance. Because VBS takes place at the same time each year, many families actually plan their vacations around it. One family that moved 180 miles from Windsor insisted that they receive an invitation to the next VBS; they planned to spend their vacation back in Windsor so that their four children could attend.

When parents preregister their child, they receive a letter from the church, stating what the church is offering their child and what they expect from the parents. Disciplinary problems are handled lovingly, but firmly. In consultation with the parents, a child may be suspended for the day, if he does not respond to the private admonition of teacher, pastor, superintendent, or helper.

After the VBS, evangelism teams call on the families that sent their children to the school. The church keeps excellent records on every child and makes the effort to contact each parent. The visits are friendly visits, conducted in a low-key manner, for the purpose of introducing the entire family to Jesus Christ. Many children have been baptized as a result, and many have joined the Sunday School and then gone on to confirmation instruction. Entire families have joined the church and become active members of the congregation, with a special concern for the VBS that had a large part in bringing them to the church. The ratio of approximately three non-member children to every one member child makes for an extremely fruitful field in which to share the Gospel.

The organization of the VBS, the enthusiasm and preparation of the leaders, and the singing are the key features during the two-week school. A 10- to 15-minute teachers' assembly follows each evening's activities. Requests, comments, and suggestions are all recorded and acted upon for the next day's classes.

The impact of summer Vacation Bible School on this congregation is staggering. A few of the many things First Lutheran did not have prior to the beginning of their VBS ministry are these: youth groups, crowded worship services, mission-mindedness, a four-vehicle bus ministry, 200 additional communicant members, a young girls choir, acolytes, a four-day mission festival, a lay minister, a vicar, people who can advertise their church, surplus funds, calls for additional Bible classes, many baptisms, and an awareness of the power of Christ. While their presence is not to be attributed entirely to the VBS, a large portion of the credit falls there. "We went, He led. We acted, He blessed," writes Pastor Krey. "He gives exceedingly more than we could ever hope for."

For those contemplating a VBS ministry or for those who want to strengthen theirs, these suggestions come from a congregation with a very successful program:

1. Make VBS a congregational tradition. Conduct it as an annual event at the same time each year.

2. Listen carefully to all comments and suggestions from each person involved.

3. Prefer mature teachers and young helpers. The teacher is the key person in VBS. Find teachers who are devoted to Christ and able to show love. Never beg someone to teach. Instead, drop the class.

4. Appreciate your staff. Compliment them at the end of each day. Support them in their efforts.

5. Provide extra helpers for nursery and kindergarten classes.

6. Treat all children and all of the staff equally. Show genuine Christian love, and love will be returned.

7. Never worry about finances. Deliver quality, and the finances will be there. You may consider asking for VBS sponsors, people who donate $2.50 per child. Many members want to be involved in VBS, but simply cannot come.

8. Ask for involvement from the congregation: prayer support, cookies for snacks, VBS sponsors, preregistrations, etc.

9. Sing! Music is the language of the heart set to rhythm. Make singing the second priority of VBS, after the teaching of God's Word.

10. Do not use gimmicks to promote VBS. It cheapens the entire program. Those drawn by gimmicks tend to be troublesome.

There is a saying at First Lutheran Church, Windsor: "God can only bless what we do, and not what, in wishful thinking, we think ought to be done." God has indeed blessed what has been done in VBS ministry at First Lutheran Church, and this activity has had an influence far beyond those two weeks in early July.

On the subject of VBS evangelism, one may wish to read the lead article of *The Evangel-Gram*, June, 1982. There one can learn of the success of Immanuel Lutheran Church, Redondo Beach, California. As a result of VBS, in 10 years time there were 34 Baptisms in the congregation, 88 new children in the Sunday School, and some parents received into membership by confirmation and reaffirmation of faith. The February 22, 1982, *Reporter*, tells of Trinity Lutheran Church in Auburn, Nebraska, and its success in VBS. Many more stories could be gathered. An excellent general resource in this area is "Evangelism Through the Vacation Bible School," by Edward F. Krueger, Bulletin No. 50179.

Christian Day School

At Timothy Lutheran Church, Chicago, the day school, the Sunday School, the Vacation Bible School, and an eight-week summer program of education are all viewed as mission opportunities for the congregation.

Parents of the unchurched children who attend one of these schools are visited by the church's evangelism callers, and as a result there were 20 children baptized at Timothy one January Sunday in 1982.

The parents of unchurched children in the day school are required to attend a series of classes to study the teachings of the church. The classes meet during the Sunday School hour on Sunday morning, a time that makes it convenient for those attending to stay another hour for worship. Other friends and relatives of unchurched children are also considered potential contacts for the church. Timothy's evangelism callers have been trained in Dialog Evangelism.[1]

"I want to go out again. I like talking about Jesus to the people," says Julie, a third-grader at Bethlehem Lutheran School, Saginaw, Michigan. Every Tuesday morning third and fourth graders are teamed up with two adult evangelism callers in order to make calls on homes in their community. The children enjoy the experience and are very willing to make up any work they missed in school that morning. Callers enjoy having the children with them and find it easier to get into people's homes.

Children participate in the preparatory Bible study, the visitation itself, and the sharing that takes place after the evangelism teams return to the church. As a result of the program, some new families are represented in the school, and the children are bolder in their witness to other children and members of their own family.[2]

These two examples demonstrate what a congregation can do, if it looks upon the day school and the weekday school as opportunities for mission. There are many other ways in which a school can build a mission mentality, some of which Kent Hunter describes in his booklet, *The Lutheran School: Opportunity for Mission!* In this booklet the author applies Church Growth principles to the Christian day school. Hunter feels that these principles can also be applied to the Sunday School, Vacation Bible School, weekday schools, etc.

A sequel to this booklet is entitled *Great Commissioning the Christian Teacher*. It is structured as a study guide for Christian education committees, school boards, day school staffs, and Bible study groups. Both booklets include discussion questions. They are available from The Church Growth Analysis and Learning Center, Corunna, Indiana 46730.

When Jesus gave the Great Commission, He intended that the entire ministry of the church be built around the goal of making disciples. Christian education for its own sake is inadequate, for no education is ever intended to be an end in itself. Christian education must be for the purpose of making disciples and enabling these disciples to reach out to others and disciple them, or it fails to measure up to our Lord's own standards.

Other resources need to be mentioned here. The Kennedy method of evangelism has been adapted to children and arranged as a teaching unit for the children in the upper elementary grades. A teachers manual and students workbook are available from Concordia Publishing House, items 1439, and 1440, under the name "Christian Witnesses." Many other resources to be mentioned in the pages to come are adaptable to the Christian day school. Note also books 8 and 10 in the *Evangelism Resource Book* on "Child Evangelism" and "Youth Evangelism" respectively. *The Evangelkit* contains many useful items for teachers and students. Edited by Edward Krueger and Jerrold Nichols, it is unfortunately now out of print.

Sunday School

The decline of the Sunday School in the mainline denominations of America has reached enormous proportions. While some denominations are experiencing growth in their Sunday Schools, most are not. Among those denominations with growing Sunday Schools are those well known for their evangelistic emphasis. However, even the Southern Baptists, an evangelistic denomination according to most observers, experienced a decline of more than 140,000 in their Sunday School enrollment over a recent four-year period.[3]

Must reading for anyone interested in evangelism and the Sunday School is the book authored by Arn, McGavran, and Arn, entitled *Growth: A New Vision for the Sunday School*. The reader will not learn about Sunday School evangelism programs, but he will find a gold mine of suggestions for improving the Sunday School, suggestions that can lead to Sunday School growth. A companion film has been produced entitled "The Great Commission Sunday School!" Both may be ordered from the Institute for American Church Growth, Suite 150, 709 East Colorado, Pasadena, California 91101.

We turn now to specific areas of the Sunday School where evangelism tools have been produced that will result in reaching people for Christ through the Sunday School.

Teacher Training

The place to begin to promote Sunday School growth is the teacher. Every teacher should be encouraged to see each student as a child who needs to experience the forgiveness of God in Jesus Christ. Teachers should be equipped to share the Gospel in a personal way with their students.

Now The Good News is a nine-session course, designed to increase the effectiveness of the witness of the Sunday School teacher. This course can help the teacher to speak her or his faith comfortably and naturally. Later on in the course, opportunity is provided for actual evangelism experiences.

A similar course in 12 sessions has been produced by the Evangelical Teacher Training Association (ETTA) entitled "Evangelize Through Christian Education," written by Elmer Towns. Write to the ETTA, 110 Bridge St., Box 327, Wheaton, Illinois 60187.

Bus Ministry

While bus ministry for Sunday Schools is a relatively rare thing among Lutherans, bus ministry for day schools, VBS, and youth programs is not. However, congregations such as Concordia Lutheran Church, San Antonio, Texas, have successfully used buses for their Sunday School ministry.

Book nine of the *Evangelism Resource Book* provides all of the information needed for starting such a ministry. Included is an extensive list of resources, books, filmstrips, periodicals, articles, etc. The Bus Ministry Pamphlet, No. 1457, and the Bus Ministry Kit, No. 1458, are also available from CPH. They contain all the record-keeping materials, doorknob hangers, invitation postcards, etc., which will be needed by the congregation that embarks upon this ministry.

Enrollment

Most denominations have some kind of enrollment program available from their publishing house. The "Sunday School Now! Campaign Kit" is one such program, available from CPH. It provides all the instructions necessary to guide a congregation through all facets of an enrollment campaign, based primarily upon the principle of children bringing their friends to Sunday School. The kit can be used for a full year's campaign, or it can be adapted for one or more months. It includes posters, postcards, planning calendar, and other promotional materials. Some congregations may want to consider writing to other denominations for sample enrollment materials.

Any congregation can adapt a community survey for the purpose of finding children in their community to attend their Sunday School (cf. Chapter 1). One organization within the LCMS that has done considerable work in this area is the Ongoing Ambassadors for Christ. They have developed a simple "Sunday School Survey" form for use within the local congregation.

Some congregations have had an annual "Bring a Friend to Sunday School Sunday" as a part of their regular emphasis upon Sunday School enrollment and Sunday School growth.

Resources

Among the many resources applicable to the Sunday School are two excellent pamphlets, "Evangelism for Sunday School Growth" by Jerrold Nichols and "Child Evangelism" by Dennis Malone. The former pamphlet is Bulletin No. 37079, available from CPH, while the latter is Book 8 in the *Evangelism Resource Book*. Nichols focuses on the Sunday School and includes ideas like the "Backyard Bible Club," which may be used as an informal way of extending the Sunday School into the community and eventually enrolling more children for Sunday mornings. Malone covers more generally the home, the day school, the church, and the community with clear application to the Sunday School, cf. also ERB, 6, B, 3.

A nondenominational organization that offers materials of all kinds to promote Sunday School growth is Arthur Davenport Associates, Inc., P.O. Box 18545, Oklahoma City, Oklahoma 73154.

Campus Crusade has several tools for sharing the Gospel with children. The "Good News Comic Book" and the "Greatest Treasure Comic Book" speak about a personal relationship with Jesus Christ in a colorful, easy-to-read format. The "Plastic Good News Glove" uses each of the fingers on the glove to communicate one part of the message of salvation. Child Evangelism Fellowship also has many useful resources for Sunday School evangelism. These will be mentioned more fully at a later time.

There are studies in print for youth, which enable them to learn about witnessing with the goal of putting this learning into practice. *Reach Out: Share Life!* is a seven-session study for high school youth from Concordia, which builds Christian community and helps youth discover ways to witness. T.I.M.E. is a 12-month program from the World Home Bible League for youth. T.I.M.E. stands for "Teens in Meaningful Evangelism." The course trains teenagers to witness using Bible correspondence courses. It is not to be confused with T.I.M.E., "Teens In Mission Encounters," from the Lutheran Bible Translators, a program designed to train young people for inreach evangelism and the support of Lutheran Bible Translators.

Puppetry

Almost any Christian bookstore will have several volumes on its shelves containing resources for use with puppets. Skits, plays, designs for making puppets, even ready-made puppets are among the things one can find at the nearby bookstore. Most major Christian publishing houses have at least some of the resources. From CPH one can order *Puppets*, a booklet by J. Graver containing activities for use in a family setting, and "Puppet Story," a four-page folder with a design for two puppets. The puppets tell the Good News by means of a story line called "Your Move." Any congregation that wants to develop this means of sharing the Gospel with children can do so with a minimum of expense and time.

There are some Christian groups that travel around the country, communicating the message of salvation through puppets and showing how congregations can begin a similar ministry. One such organization is the Salt Company, Box 465, Fairbank, Iowa 50629; another is Puppet Productions, Inc., 4343 Viewridge Ave., San Diego, California 92123.

Visitation

Many of the programs and resources already mentioned in this chapter are adaptable to an evangelism visitation program that involves children in reaching children. Another resource that can enable you to plan and carry out your own child evangelism event is the "Child Evangelism Conference." This brochure (No. 9-2286, CPH) provides the information that will enable you to have a Saturday or Sunday program of visitation to inactive Sunday School students or prospective enrollees. Materials are suggested in the brochure that will be helpful for conducting the conference.

The resource mentioned earlier, "Christian Witnesses," deserves mention again. It is a 20-lesson teaching unit for the upper elementary grades of the Christian day school, built upon the evangelism methods of D. James Kennedy. It includes study material, illustrations, songs, quizzes, and on-the-spot training activities.

Child Evangelism Fellowship

Anyone interested in learning about communicating the Gospel to children needs to be aware of the many fine resources available from Child Evangelism Fellowship, Inc., Warrenton, Missouri 63383. Child Evangelism Fellowship (CEF) was incorporated in the State of Illinois in 1937. In 1976, it moved its headquarters from Grand Rapids, Michigan, to a location just south of Warrenton, Missouri, 60 miles west of St. Louis.

"Our purpose as an interdenominational, worldwide, faith organization, composed of born-again believers, is to evangelize boys and girls with the Gospel of the Lord Jesus Christ and to establish (disciple) them in the Word of God and in the local church for Christian living."[4] CEF has about 75 full-time staff members at Warrenton, over 1000 full-time evangelists in 80 countries, and thousands of part-time workers and volunteers. They concentrate on reaching children between the ages of five and 12.

CEF was founded by J. Irvin Overholtzer, a Church of the Brethren minister, with the generous early support of Gwendolin C. Armour of the famous Chicago meat-packing family.

The two basic programs for evangelism and discipleship are the Good News Club and the 5-Day Club. Both are evangelistic in nature.

The Good News Club is conducted each school year and is held right after school for one hour a week. During that time the child learns a Bible lesson, a missionary story, songs, and visualized Bible verses. An invitation is generally given at the end of the Bible lesson, after the Gospel has been presented in simple terms. Most of the material is visualized for ease of instruction and for ease of understanding.

The 5-Day Club is a backyard Bible club held during the summer for five days, one hour a day. These are generally taught by teenagers, who have been especially trained during a two-week camp at CEF. Flashcard materials and other visualized methods are used to evangelize the children, and the local churches have an opportunity to follow up on these children.

Many of the Good News Clubs and 5-Day Clubs are held in conjunction with a local church, which provides the necessary follow-up on the entire family. There are over 8,000 Good News Clubs in operation each year.

The fellowship conducts a variety of other programs ranging from booths at county fairs to recorded telephone messages. They conduct a one-week camping program and have initiated a half-hour weekly television series, The Treehouse Club, which teaches Bible lessons and music, generously sprinkled with charm and laughter. "Here's How" is the weekly, 15-minute international radio voice of CEF, aired on more than 90 stations and providing training in winning children to Christ.

For people interested in reaching children with the Gospel, the twice annual two-week basic course, "Reaching Children Effectively," is very helpful. The bi-monthly magazine, *Evangelizing Today's Child*, is a storehouse of information, resources, and ideas, including a four-color visualized flannelgraph or flashcard lesson in each issue. A sample copy will be sent by CEF upon request.

CEF has formulated a 15-point "Statement of Faith," which affirms an inerrant Scripture in its original manuscripts and reflects a wholesome and evangelical stance on most points of doctrine. The rejection of Baptism as a means of grace must be noted, but this fact should not prevent the Lutheran from taking advantage of the many helpful programs and resources available from CEF.

"Even so it is not the will of your Father which is in heaven, that one of these little ones should perish" (Matt. 18:14 KJV).

We now turn to educational work *among adults.*

The Little Church Program

"We want people to come to church. Members don't know each other. The people aren't involved." These were the comments from leaders of Bethany Lutheran Church, Cedar Rapids, Iowa. It was to meet the needs expressed in these statements that Pastor Ron Pfluger initiated the Little Church program.

In 1978 the World Home Bible League published a 55-page booklet, entitled "The Little Church Program." The author, John DeVries, seeks to enable the church truly to be the church, not just a social gathering, by the use of small groups. These groups meet in the homes of members, and their agenda consists of five things: praise (singing and sharing reasons for praise and thanksgiving to God, prayers of praise), Bible study (20 studies are provided in the booklet), service (some specific project adopted by the group), evangelism (a trained evangelism team is assigned to each little church for reporting purposes), and world mission (each family selects, prays for, and supports its own missionary). Although changes have been made in the program, Bethany credits the guidelines of DeVries as being the inspiration for their program.

There are two options presented in the booklet for organizing the Little Church program. Leaders can organize a few pilot groups, who will meet for six months to a year, share reactions with the entire congregation, and expand the program to include others. A second option is to organize the entire church with about 20 families in each group. Bethany followed the second option, using the elders of the congregation as the leaders. DeVries encourages Little Churches to meet twice a month and for two to three hours each meeting. The Little Churches at Bethany do not meet as often or for as long a period of time.

Bethany's program is more like an elder shepherding program, but the emphasis is not on dealing with inactive members. Certainly that does occur, but the emphasis is on Christians being the church. The objective is for every member to feel he is truly a part of the church and for members to minister to one another. While there is contact with inactive members through this program, there is also the experience of joy in ministry with new members and long-time active members.

A study of Scripture was the beginning of the Little Church program at Bethany. The pastor led the elders in a study of what the church is in Scripture, what the role of elders was in the early church, and what results occurred in the Book of Acts when the church truly was the church. After months of study, prayer, and discussion, the elders divided the congregation into groups of 20 to 25 families.

At the same time, the leadership of the elders was made visible to the members of the congregation. They assisted in the distribution of the Lord's Supper, read Scripture lessons from the lectern, participated in the examination of confirmands, and the like.

The congregation was divided into 12 Little Churches. At the start, since there were only six elders, two Little Churches met together, but later these groups separated. The first meeting included a discussion of people's expectations of a minister, using a provocative piece entitled "Put Together a Perfect Minister." People realized that no minister is able to live up to all expectations. Therefore, the members themselves must also minister to one another. At that point, the Little Church program was explained to them, and it was shown how they might minister to one another through that program.

There are four major results of the Little Church program at Bethany. First, members get well acquainted with others in their Little Church. New members are automatically incorporated into a Little Church when they join Bethany, and they are thereby more easily assimilated into the life of the congregation. Some long-time active members get well acquainted for the first time. Some inactive members are also reached. One inactive member was very encouraged by the number of people from his Little Church who sent him cards during a recent hospital stay. It has been said that once a church grows beyond 80 to 100 members, no individual will be able to know all of the members well. The Little Church program enables all participants to know several families well, and that is all that any member will know in all but the smallest congregations. It can work well in a congregation of 150 communicants, and it can work just as well in a congregation of 3,000 communicants.

Second, members of these small groups pray for one another. Telephone calls inform each person of special needs and prayer requests.

As a result of such prayerful concern during a time of need, one member commented, "I would never wish anyone to be sick, but it is a way to experience something wonderful. During my stay at the hospital, the love and concern that was shown by all of you, the plants, the cards, calls, visits, and, most of all, the prayers, were unbelievable. The lady at the admittance desk told several people that my room and phone were the most popular in the hospital that week. I wish there were words to let you know how this made me feel. I can truly say I feel loved. I know the Lord heard your prayers. From the bottom of my heart let me say thanks to all of you."

Third, Little Church participants meet periodically for spiritual growth and service projects. Each year on All Saints Sunday, a meeting of all Little Churches is held at the church. During the rest of the year, the Little Churches gather on their own. Some of the meetings follow a program planned by the pastor and elders, organized around the subject of fellowship, charities, missions, evangelism, or some other congregational concern. Sometimes an elder will call his group together for a social event.

During the Lenten season, two Little Churches combine to conduct one of the Wednesday evening services. The elders receive a general outline of the service, litanies, Scripture readings, and possible hymns. Members of the Little Churches sign up to serve as greeters, ushers, acolytes, soloists, instrumentalists, readers, etc. As a result, attendance at Lenten services has doubled in the four years since the Little Church program began.

Fourth, open lines of communication are maintained with all members of Bethany through the Little Churches. Prayer requests and notice of special events are communicated by telephone to all members at least eight to 10 times a year. Through this activity many doors have been opened for pastor or elder to visit with and minister to various members.

While the danger exists for little churches to become exclusive cliques, Pastor Pfluger feels that that danger "is lessened if each of the elders and the groups understand the concepts of church and ministry...that each of the Little Churches is only a part of the body and that they build up the whole body as they function together." The regular meeting of pastor with the leaders of each Little Church also serves to diminish this danger.

The key to this program at Bethany has been the elders. Men known for their dedication to Jesus Christ have been an inspiration to others. All of the elders are enrolled in one of the Bible classes offered at Bethany. All have been asked to attend a Witness Workshop, and a number of them have participated in Dialog Evangelism. The elders meet once a month to conduct normal business, but their primary concern is to talk about the Little Church program. They share Scripture together and talk about the joys and difficulties of the Little Church program, as well as possible solutions to those difficulties.

It is the responsibility of the elders to get to know the people in their Little Church. They call on all families, including shut-ins, new members, the hospitalized, and families they do not personally know. They have agreed to make a minimum of one contact per week, whether that be by phone, home visit, conversation after church services, lunch together, or some other way.

"I feel you can take a program and tell people, 'Here it is, do it!'," writes Pastor Pfluger, "or you can try to understand where the people are and meet them there. Don't ask them to do more than they are prepared to do. Gradually lead them to grow their own program." This is happening at Bethany.

The emphasis at Bethany is not on a set of materials. The emphasis is on the people being the church. Christians can and must show spiritual and physical concern for one another. That concern is more easily shown when people have a smaller group on which to concentrate.

Pastor Pfluger states, "Through the Little Church program, through prayers requested for one another, through the times they meet together to talk things over with each other and their elders, through the phone callers who inform them of events in the congregation, through the contacts by telephone and personal visits, and through concern shown by elders and other members of the group, we are seeking to build up one another in the faith and eventually get more and more of the members to recognize their gifts and use them in the ministry God has given them."

Church attendance has risen from an average of 277 in 1978, the year the program was introduced, to 328 in 1982. Members are becoming much better acquainted, not only with those in their Little Church, but also with others. New members are now becoming involved as soon as they join the church, and some inactive members have begun to worship.

While the Little Church program was not undertaken at Bethany with the idea of being an evangelistic program, there were membership gains as a result. As members got to know and care for one another, as the body of Christ at Bethany became healthier, many outside the congregation were attracted. The members themselves were more conscious of inviting others to visit their church. Pastor Pfluger writes, "The Little Churches have done much to help foster an evangelistic attitude. This attitude . . . has greatly enhanced our outreach program." Congregations that consciously make it their objective to invite unchurched friends and relatives to the Little Churches will find the program to be effective in reaching people for Jesus Christ.

Home Bible Study Resources

Since the Little Church program is a home Bible study program, little more needs to be said about home Bible study as a tool for evangelistic outreach. However, some additional resources will prove helpful to those persons considering the development of such a ministry.

Two books by the same author will provide a great deal of information. Albert J. Wollen is the author of *How to Conduct Home Bible Classes* (Scripture Press) and *Miracles Happen in Group Bible Study* (G/L Regal Books). These two books provide bibliographies for further reading in addition to the practical information in the text.

The Board for Parish Services of the LCMS has published Information Bulletin 60874 on this subject, entitled "Have You Tried a Home Bible Study Group?". An excellent article by Marilyn Kunz, associate director and co-founder of Neighborhood Bible Studies, Inc., appeared in *Christianity Today*, entitled "Bible Studies that Bring Them to Belief."[5] Kunz has also co-authored a booklet with Catherine Schell, *How to Start a Neighborhood Bible Study*. For a copy write to Neighborhood Bible Studies, Dobbs Ferry, New York 10522. Book 6. B of the *Evangelism Resource Book* is devoted to evangelism through Bible study groups. An additional resource from the Lutheran Church in America is the Koinonia Institute. Write to the Division for Parish Services, 2900 Queen Lane, Philadelphia, Pennsylvania 19129.

Lutheran Tape Ministry

A catalog of more than 300 cassette tapes, many of them useful as evangelism resources, is available by writing to Lutheran Tape Ministry, Inc. (LTM), 124 S. 24th St., Suite 202, Omaha, Nebraska 68102.

LTM is the brainchild of the Rev. Fred Naumann, who has been making these tapes available for more than a decade. Naumann emphasizes verse-by-verse Bible study. An estimated audience of nearly 200,000 listened to one or more LTM tapes in 1981. A corps of 35 volunteers assists Pastor Naumann in making these tapes available.

The Gospel is presented in many of the tapes, some of them geared specifically to children, youth, or the aged. Some of the tapes are useful as follow-up material for the new Christian. Others can be used in the training of evangelism callers, such as cassette #160 on forgiveness, tapes

#136-139 on the emptiness of materialism, and tapes #166-168 on witnessing and evangelism by Erwin J. Kolb, Edward A. Westcott, Jr., Ted A. Raedeke, and Eugene H. Vetter.

Pastor Naumann's wife Dorothy lists some of the ways in which tapes can be useful as evangelism resources:

— to educate, enlighten and inspire evangelism callers;

— to leave with a prospect to help answer their questions;

— to use in family devotions, teen devotions, and for German speaking people;

— to leave a children's tape or "How to study the Bible" tape with a prospective family;

— to give a child a gift of one of the children's tapes for bringing another child to Sunday School regularly.[6]

Innovative thinkers will be able to dream up other uses for cassette tapes for evangelistic outreach.

Congregational Evangelism Opportunities

Other opportunities exist within the Christian congregation for reaching adults with the Gospel of Jesus Christ. The pastor's class can be viewed not only as an opportunity for making visits on prospective members, but also as a time in which the Gospel is clearly presented, cf. ERB, 6. B. 2. Vacation Bible School has involved the entire family, adults included, in some congregations, by having VBS during the evening hours. Adult Bible classes on Sundays and on other days of the week can have appropriate discussion from time to time on God's plan for man's salvation. Church libraries ought to be equipped with several volumes that tell the story of Jesus' mission on earth.

One other area of ministry that can be included here is the ministry of a congregation to its inactive members. Many of those whose membership is held in a Christian church do not have a saving relationship with Jesus Christ. It is the church's responsibility to share the Gospel with these people so that they may come to confess Christ as Savior and recommit themselves to their Christian life within the church.

In most congregations, this aspect of a church's ministry is the responsibility of the elders and pastor. There are many program helps in most denominations designed to enable congregations to organize for effective inreach to its members. "The Shepherding Program" of the LCA is one such program. "Regaining the Straying" of the WELS is another such program, which is designed to be used in conjunction with "Talk About the Savior," a program of evangelism visitation mentioned in Chapter I. Any congregation can divide its families into zones, assign one zone to each elder, train its elders to share the Gospel, and then ask that the elders begin visiting inactive members for the purpose of evangelizing those members who are spiritually lost.

Many of the resources now available on assimilating members into the life of a congregation and closing the back door of the church to membership losses also deal with this important area of ministry. *Assimilating New Members* by Lyle Schaller (Abingdon Press), *The Caring System* by L. Ray Sells and Donald LaSuer (Christian Communication), and *Your Church Has Doors: How to Open the Front and Close the Back* by Kent Hunter (the Church Growth Analysis and Learning Center) are important resources in this area.

Additional resources that merit attention are Book 7. C. of the *Evangelism Resource Book* and "Inreach Evangelism" by Jerrold Nichols, No. 9-2319 from the Board for Evangelism Services (BFES). Section X on "Assimilation" and Section XI on "Conservation" in the old ERB are also worth reading, as are "Elders at Work" by Elmer Kettner (Concordia) and "Reclaiming Souls for Christ" by Herman Gockel (BFES). Finally, note the volume appearing in the present series by Alan Harre.

Chapter 5

The Marketplace Approach

In this chapter we will cover those types of evangelism approaches and programs that seek to present the Gospel to people wherever they are—that is, in the marketplace. We meet people at our place of work, on vacations, at meetings of community organizations, and over the backyard fence. Many of the people who will never participate in some evangelism program of the congregation can learn to share their faith in the marketplace.

Perhaps the word "witness" would be a better word to use in this chapter than "evangelism." There are programs and resources available that can train Christians to witness by word of mouth and the printed page. Witness is that evangelistic activity which takes place in a natural, spontaneous manner. Training for witness may occur, but witness is here distinguished from those activities that occur in structured evangelism programs.

Having said that, there are some evangelism programs and resources in this chapter that do not fit that model precisely. They defy categorization. They could easily fit into several categories, but they are included here because they fit most easily into the marketplace approach.

Witness Workshop

According to Ephesians 4:11, God gave "some to be evangelists," but according to Acts 1:8 and other passages, all Christians are witnesses. While many of the programs in the preceding pages, particularly those discussed in Chapter I, are designed for people with gifts in evangelism, the information presented in this chapter is for all Christians. Not all Christians are evangelists, but all Christians are witnesses. Therefore, congregations need to provide opportunities for the vast majority of their members, not gifted in evangelism, to enhance their witness life. The Witness Workshop is one of those opportunities, and St. Paul Lutheran Church, Trenton, Michigan, is one of those congregations. A Gospel Communication Clinic helps you develop a witness to a specific person, probably a close friend. A witness workshop helps you respond in word and/or deed to *any* person, situation, event, statement, experience, or activity.

In 1974 Wayne Pohl became administrative pastor of St. Paul, bringing Church Growth principles with him to a plateaued congregation. These principles led the congregation, four years later, to call Michael Malinsky to serve the congregation as pastor in charge of evangelism, with additional responsibilities in hospital visitation and teaching.

With the arrival of Malinsky came an emphasis upon training people to be witnesses. Evangelism conjured up in the minds of many people thoughts of sweaty-palmed confrontations with complete strangers. The distinction mentioned above between evangelists and witnesses served to relieve many Christians of guilt feelings they had because they were not making evangelism calls on people. At the same time, it taught the members of St. Paul that each Christian has many natural, God-given opportunities to share the message of the Gospel with friends and relatives.

A witness workshop was developed in which many members of the congregation were trained to witness. In the years between 1979 and 1983, approximately 400 members of the congregation attended such a workshop, held from 9:30 a.m. to 3:30 p.m. on a Saturday. Workshops were later cut down to four hours on a Saturday, and then to three hours on a Thursday evening, in order to draw additional people. The workshops are held quarterly, one or two weeks after the quarterly pastor's class, so that new members can be encouraged to attend and develop their skills in witnessing.

A typical three-hour workshop introduces the subject of witnessing, with a special focus on *oikos* (the New Testament Greek word for "house, household, family") evangelism. The word *oikos* in the New Testament refers not only to immediate family members, but also to slaves, grandparents, and others living at the same address, as well as other relatives. Members of St. Paul learn how to identify those people in their *oikos*, "household" or extended family, people who are their friends and relatives. They are equipped with simple, practical ways to share their faith with these people. An hour of the time is devoted to small group sharing, a time during which participants actually witness to one another by sharing their testimonies.

The advanced workshop will use another three hours to focus on four areas: (1) how to share the Gospel with another person; (2) how to deal effectively with objections; (3) how to be a better listener; and (4) how to illustrate Scripture truth.

Pastor Malinsky lists eight positive changes that have occurred in the congregation as a result of the workshops:

1. An increased number of evangelism callers. During the years of the witness workshops, the number of people involved in evangelism visitation increased from eight to more than 25. Many of these evangelists first became interested in evangelism by attending a witness workshop.

2. An increase of spontaneous witnessing. Many unchurched people in the community have said that a member of St. Paul has been witnessing to them, and many of them have become members. The number of adult confirmands in the church has increased steadily from 37 in 1978 (the year before witness workshops began) to 144 in 1982. In that five-year span, 433 adults were confirmed.

3. Members called to full-time ministry. Thirteen members of the congregation have answered the call to full-time ministry. "Virtually all of them were lay men and women who pulled up their roots, quit jobs, and went the way of Abraham," writes Pastor Malinsky. "Most of these people have been heavily involved in witnessing and evangelism."

4. Increased Bible study. When members witnessed to friends who were Mormons or Jehovah's Witnesses, they realized that they needed to know their Bible better. A small group discipleship training began in 1983 to help members become more thoroughly versed in their faith and able to defend it.

5. Expanded mailing ministry. A monthly mailing was begun early in 1982 for all people considered prospects for membership. Initially the mailings were sent only to visitors, but the program was later expanded to include people referred by members of the congregation. Every three months a bulletin insert serves as a referral sheet, which members can use to list names and addresses of friends. The promise is made *not* to visit these referrals, unless they first visit the church or unless the member gives permission.

6. Increased programming for the unchurched. "As our members have changed in their attitudes toward witnessing, they have developed more programs to include the unchurched," comments Malinsky. "For

instance, when we had a stress seminar last year, 80 percent of our attendees were non-members. A similar response was seen at our singles' ministry's divorce recovery workshop."

7. Openness to specialized staff ministries. This openness includes not only two pastors, but also four full-time lay ministers. Since the lay people understand that not all are evangelists, they realize that not all staff members are gifted to lead in every area of ministry. Art Beyer helps members discover their spiritual gifts. He also develops child education programs at St. Paul. In 1981, Ron Wrightson was called to manage and develop the shared group life and to incorporate new members into the life of the church. That same year, Paul Krentz was called to develop a youth ministry with teens and young adults. In 1982, Bill Heide came on staff as director of music.

Malinsky notes, "At this time we are feeling the need for a full-time counselor-mercy man and eventually a full-time director of singles. When our people witness to their unchurched friends, they can feel confident that their church can meet their needs: physical, emotional, and spiritual."

8. Witness of new Christians. The longer a person is a Christian, the fewer non-Christians he knows. Church Growth people have long known this important principle. In recognition of this important fact, the final session of the pastor's class introduces the subject of *oikos* evangelism. Names and addresses of unchurched acquaintances are added to the mailing list. The new members are encouraged at that time to attend the quarterly witness workshop.

Members are just as enthusiastic about the witness workshops as are the staff. One member commented, "I learned things I never imagined before." Another illustrated the first change in the congregation mentioned above, "God used the workshop to get me committed to be an evangelist." A third complained that the workshop was too short, and a fourth said, "The workshop motivated me to study my Bible more thoroughly."

Since 75 to 90 percent of those who join churches do so because of the influence of a friend or relative, the implementation of a concept similar to the Witness Workshops at Trenton, Michigan, is a must for every congregation serious about the Great Commission.

In 1981 the Board for Evangelism Services of the LCMS produced a manual, four years in the making, entitled "Witness Workshop." While this manual was not contributed to by the people at Trenton, nor is it the manual in use there, many of the same concepts appear both in this manual and in the materials utilized at St. Paul Lutheran Church.

Designed for eight hours of teaching and interaction, the witness workshop can be taught over a Friday evening and Saturday, for two hours each night on four consecutive midweek evenings, or by means of some other suitable schedule.

The manual provides all of the resources necessary for planning and teaching a witness workshop. Enough material is included to enable the presenter to teach three, four, or five workshops without repeating any of the materials. Sample transparencies, Bible studies, film suggestions, schedules, dramas, discussion guides, and the like, along with all the necessary information to organize a witness workshop committee, are a part of the manual. The workshop may be adapted for use with or without visitation during the workshop hours.

The Master's Plan for Making Disciples

"The Master's Plan is the most effective way I know to bring people to Jesus Christ. It has Biblical and historical integrity. The ideas work and our church is growing." So says LCMS Pastor Stephen Wagner, of Prince of Peace Lutheran Church, Carrollton, Texas.

Based on a book by the same title, "The Master's Plan for Making Disciples" is a rediscovery of the New Testament strategy for evangelism and disciple-making. It has been demonstrated from Scripture and down through the centuries that the Christian message travels best over the natural bridges of close human relationships, or "webs," the *oikos* mentioned in the previous pages.

While the authors, Win Arn and Charles Arn, would react against calling the Master's Plan a program, it can be considered an evangelism program. However, we must hasten to add that it is also much more. It is a process by which a Christian can develop a life-style through which he organizes his time, resources, and energy into an intentional yet natural disciple-making plan. There is no memorized presentation; there are no rehearsed questions and answers. There is no structured visitation.

In nine hours of training, Christians learn the seven steps of the program and the principles that undergird these steps. Step 1 is to identify your friends and relatives whom you might be able to reach. Step 2 is to develop a personal profile on those individuals. In Step 3 you begin to pray regularly and specifically for these people. In Step 4 you focus your efforts on one or more of these people. Step 5 shows you how to develop a plan for reaching this person. In Step 6 you learn to strengthen your witness. Attendance at a witness workshop would be useful for this purpose. Step 7 is the incorporation of the new member into the body of Christ.

In the local congregation, the training leader meets with participants in the Master's Plan training sessions for three meetings of two-and-a-half to three hours each. A series of overhead transparencies is provided in the church's materials, and congregations have free use of a videotape that has been produced for use in conjunction with the training sessions. The Bible study materials and exercises in the participant's workbook produce good interaction between leader and participants. The leader's materials are easy to follow, clear and simple enough for most people to use.

The pastor should be the trainer for the first series of training meetings, but a lay leader may become the Master's Plan coordinator and lead subsequent training sessions. Following the training meetings, participants form support teams, which meet twice a month so that members of these teams can pray together, talk about progress in their witness, and discuss how best to proceed. Ideas and suggestions shared in these meetings help to encourage Christians to continue their efforts to reach the people in their "web" of influence. The meetings also provide a sense of accountability, with the result that participants more consciously work on their disciple-making plan.

The Master's Plan is Biblical, natural, relatively easy to implement, and worth every penny that a congregation will invest in it. In the years to come, Rev. Wagner's comments will prove to be true for large numbers of congregations. The Master's Plan has broad application to rural, small town, inner city, suburban, and apartment ministries. Any place where people live in contact with other people, the Master's Plan can be effective.

Tract Ministry

The congregation or individual interested in expanding its witness through evangelistic tracts should begin by viewing the filmstrip, "One Great Word Above the Din," a Concordia Production made available by Aid Association for Lutherans (AAL), a fraternal life insurance company. In this filmstrip, the possibilities of tract use are explained, and the viewer sees how to get involved in a tract ministry. While Concordia Tract Mission (CTM) is featured in the filmstrip, the ministry of tract distribution is not limited to CTM. The application of the principles learned in the filmstrip goes far beyond the ministry of one tract society.

The Leaders Guide for the filmstrip lists six programs of tract evangelism:

1. Placement and maintenance of a *tract rack* in the narthex of the church, in the lobby of a local hospital, or in another suitable location.

2. An organized program of *individual tract distribution*, perhaps a program that sets as its initial goal the distribution of one tract a day per person.

3. *A neighborhood evangelism canvass.*

4. An organized program of *including tracts* in envelopes *when paying bills* by mail.

5. An organized program of *including tracts in greeting cards* of all kinds.

6. *participation in the Paper Peace Corps* project by an auxiliary organization or by the entire congregation.

The Paper Peace Corps is a program that encourages Christians to collect outdated religious literature—old Bibles, Sunday School lessons, etc.—to send to missions and partner churches overseas where the English language is understood.

The "One Great Word" of the filmstrip is this: "Jesus died and rose again." The din above which this one great word seeks to be heard is ". . . the din of humanity and conflict."

Viewers are reminded that Adoniram Judson, one of the first Christian missionaries to Burma, was converted through the message of a Christian tract. The 95 Theses of Martin Luther were printed in tract form. Tracts are in print that are relevant to virtually every need, many languages, and each age group.

In one of the CTM tracts, "Ten Tips for Tract Users," some practical hints for the distribution of tracts are given. These suggestions are reprinted under the title "Using Tracts" in Book 14. D. of the *Evangelism Resource Book*.

Any tract society will provide a free catalog of its tract listings to anyone who writes for it. Among the more well-known tract societies are Concordia Tract Mission, Box 201, St. Louis, Missouri 63166; American Tract Society, P.O. Box 402008, Garland, Texas 75040; Canadian Tract Society (the Canadian affiliate of the American Tract Society), P.O. Box 203, Port Credit, Mississauga, Ontario L5G 4L7; Faith, Prayer & Tract League, 2627 Elmridge Dr. N.W., Grand Rapids, Michigan 49504; Good News Publishers, 9825 W. Roosevelt Rd., Westchester, Illinois 60153; American Bible Society, 1865 Broadway, New York, New York 10023; and Arthur Davenport Associates, Inc., P.O. Box 18545, Oklahoma City, Oklahoma 73154.

The World Home Bible League produces several tracts for evangelistic purposes, and the BFES of the LCMS has produced several tracts on the message of salvation, some of them available also in Spanish, cf. "Evangelism Catalog." Pins and pocket crosses are another form of a tract, some of which are listed in the "Evangelism Catalog" and the *Evangelism Resource Book*, Book 14. F.

Fair Ministry

The possibilities for a witness ministry at a county or state fair or community festival are limited only by the imagination of those who do the planning. Such a ministry would probably center around a booth and include distribution of tracts and other printed literature, coupled with verbal and visual witness to Christ. Bibles, New Testaments, Scripture portions, and correspondence courses can be among the literature distributed at the booth. In some cases the planning and reservation of space may have to begin a year or more in advance.

In 1981 the Arizona State Fair in Phoenix was the location of a witness booth in which more than 100 Lutheran Christians participated. For the past nine years the Lutheran Evangelism Association—Prayer Family International has organized and sponsored a "Christian Witness Booth" in cooperation with the Lutheran churches in Arizona.

People from these congregations staffed the booth, with three-hour shifts, two people per shift, four shifts a day for 17 days. The Invitational Booklet, designed like a double postcard, has the way of salvation printed on one side, with the other side to be torn off and mailed in for a free home Bible study course from Project Philip, a New Testament, other information, or a personal visit. Over 12,000 of these booklets were distributed in 1981, while hundreds of New Testaments, Scripture portions, and tracts were distributed.[1]

The same criticism voiced in regard to the "Here's Life" campaign may be repeated here. While Campus Crusade measured the success of "Here's Life" by the number of decisions recorded, others measure the success of a program by the number of tracts, Scripture portions, or correspondence courses distributed. While this criticism does not invalidate the results nor suggest that attempts at literature distribution not be made, it reminds believers that God's standard is disciples, not decisions or distributions. This fact encourages Christians to work on the follow-up that should take place after literature distribution.

Pastor Erv Rasmussen, director of the Lutheran Evangelism Association, did most of the training the first year, but in later years those with experience in previous fairs did much of the training. See below for more information on the Lutheran Evangelism Association.

Campgrounds and Vacationers

There are a variety of materials available for individual families who want to witness as they travel, or for congregations which wish to witness to those who travel in their area, particularly for those congregations located in tourist areas.

The *Evangelism Resource Book* has five suggestions for congregations that are located in such areas:

1) hold services at convenient times, perhaps even extra services;

2) conduct special services at places where the setting is both more informal and more conveniently located near camp sites;

3) advertise services, emphasizing that these are "come as you are" services;

4) arrange gatherings at camp sites or resort areas for group singing, movies, discussions, and the distribution of tracts and pamphlets;

5) arrange Vacation Bible School activities for the children at resort areas;[2]

Congregations are also invited to consult with the Committee on Leisure Ministries of the LCMS Board for Parish Services.

For individual families, the Lutheran Laymen's League offers a pocket-sized booklet entitled "Outdoor Ministry Manual." It contains suggestions for the worship and devotional life of campers and vacationers, orders of worship, songs and hymns, etc. While it does not contain suggestions for witness to one's faith in Christ, it does provide some ideas for worship services which individual families might like to have and to which these families could invite fellow vacationers.

Almost any devotional aid or songbook would be suitable for use on vacation. Some titles, however, relate specifically to camping and vacationing. *Christ in Our Vacation* is a collection of daily devotions from Augsburg Publishing House. *Family Vacation Idea Book*, by Harold Belgum, is a Concordia publication. *Wonder in God's Wilderness*, by Samuel Schmiechen, is available from Augsburg.

Numerous tracts may be used for distribution, two of which caught this author's eye. "Vacation Aids" is a tract containing seven short meditations on vacation themes. It is available from the Faith, Prayer & Tract League, Grand Rapids, Michigan 49504. Another title is from Concordia Tract Mission, entitled "How to Conduct Family Worship."

Many of the same evangelism programs and principles enunciated elsewhere will be helpful to the Christian, who wishes to enhance his witness among vacationers, as he meets them in this part of the marketplace.

Prison Ministry

This section deals with the first of several approaches to evangelism that might best be titled "Special Needs in the Marketplace."

A series of articles in *The Evangel-Gram* alerts us to the evangelistic potential of ministry to those in prison.[3] The first article chronologically talks about evangelism by correspondence with prisoners. Project Philip correspondence courses are suggested as possible tools, in addition to the friendship and personal letters of the writer. Persons interested in corresponding with a prisoner may write to one of several organizations:

Christian Prison Volunteers
"Visit-By-Mail"
Box 1949
Hollywood, California 90028

Prison Fellowship
P. O. Box 40562
Washington, D.C. 20016

International Lutheran Laymen's League
Mail Counseling Department
2185 Hampton Avenue
St. Louis, Missouri 63139

The second article is written by Allen Hanson, a Lutheran Christian who served a nine-month sentence at Minnesota State Prison at Stillwater in 1978. He writes on the subject of "Christian Prison Visitation," including a very helpful list of "Do's and Don'ts." Hanson mentions the limited educational background of a large percentage of prison inmates as a frequent hindrance to correspondence. He suggests that a telephone call or a personal visit, arranged through an established prison service organization, is the best approach.

In the third article, Hanson talks about the four opportunities for witness: the county jail, the family of the prisoner, the state or federal penitentiary, and the ex-offender. He reminds us of the importance of this kind of ministry when he quotes from the New Testament, "Remember those in prison as if you were their fellow prisoners." (Heb. 13:3 NIV)

Something more needs to be written about one of the organizations whose address is given above—Prison Fellowship (PF). Organized in 1977 by former counsel to President Nixon, Charles W. Colson, Prison Fellowship has become the most effective ministry to the prisoners of our country. In 1981 Prison Fellowship was active in 209 state, federal, county, and municipal prisons, affecting the lives of more than 12,300 inmates, 2,000 families of prisoners, and 1,250 ex-offenders, who were enrolled in Prison Fellowship programs.

Through the assistance of more than 8,400 volunteers, Prison Fellowship has been able to form local Care Committees. "Care Committees are structured to pool the resources of local churches and communities to meet the needs of those they serve. In 1981 25 state and regional directors, coordinated by PF field director and ex-offender Paul Kramer, worked with 141 Care Committees in 35 different states."[4]

In-prison seminars provide opportunities for spiritual birth and spiritual growth among inmates, while helping to bridge the gap between prison and community. In-community seminars take inmates into local churches and schools for fellowship and ministry. Atlanta was the site of a two-week experiment during which six inmates from a Florida prison were brought into the community to insulate the houses of two elderly ladies. Local Christian families housed the men, the local media followed the event closely, and a real bond was established between the inmates and the people they helped.

National commentator Paul Harvey told his listeners that this experiment could become a model for other alternative means of punishment for nonviolent offenders. Indeed, this is one of the goals of PF—to discuss such alternatives with the appropriate people and help public officials deal with the overcrowding, violence, and skyrocketing costs of prisons.

PF maintains a prayer chain, publishes a variety of printed materials, and is extending its ministry into other countries. Probably the most important aspect of PF is the coordination of the work of volunteers, who are interested in writing to an inmate, visiting on a regular basis, helping coordinate programs, or in some way working with inmates, their families, and their communities in this type of ministry.

PF is certainly correct when it states that prisons do not "cure" criminals. Only God can do that. Christians who want to serve in this area of ministry should not fail to contact Prison Fellowship.

Teen Challenge

Another special need in the marketplace is the need for freedom from drug and alcohol abuse. Few organizations come with higher recommendations than Teen Challenge. Words of glowing tribute have come from Ronald Reagan, Charles Colson, Billy and Ruth Graham, and others. Art Linkletter has said, "In my opinion, Teen Challenge is doing the best all-around job of providing the kids with something meaningful in their lives."[5]

The most impressive commendation, however, is from Dr.

Catherine Hess, study director for the United States Health, Education, & Welfare Department. In a 1976 study done by HEW, Dr. Hess stated that cure rates normally run at about one to ten percent, whereas she found the cure rate of Teen Challenge to be 86 percent. This percentage is based on those interviewed five years after completing the Teen Challenge program. She also found that 70 percent of the graduates of Teen Challenge programs were working in a productive field. These and other statistics led her to say, "There is no question in my mind that the Teen Challenge Program is the most successful one I have ever seen."[6] Dr. John A. Howard, member of the National Commission on Marijuana and Drug Abuse, echoes the sentiments of Dr. Hess, "Of all the drug programs reported to the Commission, the most successful is the religiously based program conducted by Teen Challenge."

Teen Challenge is based on four principles:

1) There is hope for a person with life-controlling problems.

2) Sin, not drugs, alcohol, etc., is the major root problem.

3) The only cure for sin and its symptoms (drugs, alcohol, etc.) is Jesus Christ.

4) Jesus Christ, living within a person, takes the desire for sin out of that person's life.[7]

There are 98 centers in the U.S. and over 150 worldwide, where Teen Challenge is at work. Troubled persons can come in for initial counseling and an interview. If the person is willing to accept the rules of the center, and if the center accepts him, then the person begins a program of 6 to 12 weeks at the induction center with 6 to 20 other people. All drugs, alcohol, and cigarettes are taken away, and the individual begins a program that includes daily work, Bible study, recreation time, and other normal daily activities. Upon the successful completion of this phase of the program, the person is transferred to a farm for 10 months to work with 50 to 200 others. There, more work, more Bible study, and the learning of a trade take place, while the individual learns love, self-esteem, character, and the value of hard work and worship.

Teen Challenge normally works with men between the ages of 17 and 30, although work is also being done with juveniles under 17 and with women. The program has recently been expanded to include behavioral problems as well as drug and alcohol abuse.

Teen Challenge began in 1958 as a result of the efforts of the Rev. David Wilkerson in New York City. Although Wilkerson is no longer directly involved in the work of Teen Challenge, he remains supportive of it. Teen Challenge is a department under the Division of Home Missions of the Assemblies of God, 1445 Boonville, Springfield, Missouri

65802. The national representative of the program is Frank Reynolds. It is included in this book because part of its ministry is the communication of the Gospel of Jesus Christ to those enrolled in its program. Because of the affiliation of Teen Challenge with the Assemblies of God, the baptism of the Holy Spirit is a part of its program. This baptism is considered an important, though not absolutely essential, part of its program. It is not pushed upon its people, and it is mentioned up front during initial contacts with those desiring to become a part of the Teen Challenge program.

The story of Teen Challenge is told in a 45-minute film called "The Jesus Factor" and in a 174-page book by the same title, authored by David Manuel with Don Wilkerson and Reginald Yake (Logos International).

Jews for Jesus, etc.

"The people least likely to be evangelized are those who offer some resistance," said Moishe Rosen in a telephone conversation. He went on to say that the church tends to back down in such cases. This is where other organizations can step in. In many cases, a specialized organization is needed in order to reach a specific group, what Church Growth people call a homogeneous unit. Jews for Jesus is such an organization.

The Jews for Jesus ministry (JFJ) was founded in 1973 with eight staff members and a mailing list "formed by pooling our Christmas card lists," the leaflets say. Today there are 45 on staff, four of these located at the San Francisco headquarters at 60 Haight St., 94102. The Christmas card lists have grown. "Virtually every Jew in the United States has now heard of Jews for Jesus," says Sue Perlman, the organization's information officer.[8]

Rosen describes the ministry of Jews for Jesus as a tactical ministry of strategic evangelism. Specific tools and strategies are employed to create an overall impression in a community. Newspaper ads are frequently purchased, street preaching occurs, and broadsides (imaginative, humorous Christian tracts with a Jewish flavor) are distributed, sometimes as many as 50,000 in 24 hours. Since the beginning of Jews for Jesus, over 25 million broadsides have been distributed. Parades, picket lines, and other highly visible strategies are also used.

Each summer since 1974, Jews for Jesus has taken teams of people to New York City for a six- to ten-week evangelism campaign, utilizing all of these methods. They have a goal of raising the issue of Jesus in the Jewish community and obtaining names and addresses of interested individuals whom they meet on the streets, both Jew and Gentile. As a matter of fact, "although the campaign's target is the Jewish population, about ten Gentiles become Christians through the ministry of Jews for Jesus for every Jew who accepts Christ."[9] Jews who respond to the ministry of JFJ receive a free subscription to *Issues*, JFJ's bi-monthly evangelistic publication.

There are five permanent branches with more such locations being planned as centers for missionary outreach. San Francisco, Los Angeles, New York City, Chicago, and Toronto are the current branches. To those areas of the country where there are not enough Jewish people to sustain a branch, JFJ sends individual missionaries on special tours and mobile evangelistic teams, which travel regularly throughout the country and sometimes abroad. These teams include the Liberated Wailing Wall (the music team) and the New Jerusalem Players (the drama group). As they travel, they tell about the Jews for Jesus ministry in host churches, and they have ample opportunity for evangelism on campuses and street corners.

Special banquets and Jewish evangelism seminars are regularly held in key cities. A new program of volunteer workers will help raise an ongoing testimony to Jewish people in cities where no JFJ branch exists.

Jews for Jesus are evangelical in the best sense of the word. That is, they are both involved in the presentation of the "Evangel," the Good News of salvation through faith in Jesus Christ, and they hold to the complete authority and trustworthiness of the Bible.

There are some elements of decision theology in JFJ writings, but the concerned reader will be intelligent enough to compensate for it in his use of such materials.

Unlike many other evangelism programs and agencies, Jews for Jesus have specific goals in any outreach program. They carefully evaluate the results, and they scrap methods and programs that do not achieve a certain minimum level of success. Other Christians would do well to imitate this aspect of the JFJ work, in congregations, in agencies, and in other types of evangelistic work.

Among the most valuable JFJ resources for witness to Jews are the book *Share the New Life with a Jew*, by Moishe and Ceil Rosen (Moody), the booklet "How to Witness Simply and Effectively to the Jews," by Moishe Rosen, published by Jews for Jesus, and *Y'shua, the Jewish Way to Say Jesus*, by Moishe Rosen.

There are numerous other organizations that carry out a ministry designed to reach Jews with the Gospel. Among them are the American Board of Missions to the Jews, 236 W. 72nd St., New York, New York 10023; Aedus Testimony Center, 6057 N. Kedzie Ave., Chicago, Illinois

60659; American Messianic Fellowship, 7448 N. Damen Ave., Chicago, Illinois 60645; B'rit Shalom, P.O. Box 223, Highland, Illinois 60035. A pan-Lutheran organization is Good News for Israel, Box 23018, Richfield, Minnesota 55423.

Within the LCMS mention must be made of the Lutheran Institute for Jewish Evangelism (LIJE), headed by director Rev. Bruce J. Lieske. Lieske is a former member of the Committee for Witnessing to Jewish People (LCMS) and author of the committee's major publication, *Witnessing to Jewish People*. LIJE offers a correspondence course in Jewish evangelism and other materials. Tracts, a Bible study course, a filmstrip, and other materials may be ordered directly from the LCMS Board for Evangelism Services at 1333 S. Kirkwood Rd., St. Louis, Missouri 63122.

Lutheran Discipleship Ministry

Lutheran Discipleship Ministry (LDM) was organized by Bob and Linda Skulte in 1974 after seven years with Campus Crusade, because they wanted to work within their own denomination, The Lutheran Church—Missouri Synod.

The objectives of LDM are two: to disciple lay people so that they may have a more consistent daily walk with Jesus Christ and thus share the Gospel more effectively; to train and mobilize lay people for the purpose of building a growing church.

Over a 20-week period of time in a congregation, the Skultes focus their attention on three primary ministries: establishing an ongoing intercessory prayer ministry, establishing ongoing home discipleship studies, and establishing ongoing spiritual life retreats.

The first of these ministries is established primarily through a six-hour, one-day workshop on prayer. The second and third are accomplished through two weekends, usually three weeks apart. The first is a fellowship weekend, intended to stimulate interest in fellowship with other Christians and in a growing spiritual life. The weekend lays the groundwork for the second weekend, the spiritual life retreat. As a result of the fellowship weekend, members begin to participate in home discipleship studies, 10 weeks of studies led by pre-trained congregational leaders.

The spiritual life retreat assists lay people in trusting the ministry of the Holy Spirit in their lives and in developing a more consistent daily Christian walk. It also encourages people to participate in both inreach and outreach programs of the congregation.

One can learn from LDM the fact that many Christians do not

witness because the level of their spiritual life needs lifting. Once they receive proper spiritual feeding, a life of witness will occur much more spontaneously. The emphasis upon one's devotional life is well taken. LDM also emphasizes the priesthood of all believers in a very practical way, not only by teaching this concept of discipleship, but also by working directly with lay people to achieve this kind of discipleship.

Bob and Linda Skulte can be contacted at 577 Seventeenth Ave. NW, New Brighton, Minnesota 55112. They are graduates of Valparaiso University with Religion and Theology majors. The ministry is directed by a Board of Directors of LCMS laymen and pastors.

Lutheran Youth Encounter

Lutheran Youth Encounter (LYE) is a relational youth ministry, which seeks to evangelize unchurched youth and to restore inactive baptized youth of the church to a meaningful Christian faith. In addition to these objectives, LYE seeks to nurture Christian youth and equip them to serve Christ with their witness and their total Christian life. "The purpose of Lutheran Youth Encounter is to contribute to the life and mission of the universal Christian church by communicating the Good News of Jesus Christ from the perspective of the Lutheran confessional tradition."[10] This purpose is carried out among Lutherans of various denominations in different ways.

LYE congresses of 500 to 3,000 persons are sponsored in many locations throughout the U.S. each year. During these weekends, Christian leaders of national prominence join with local pastors, lay people, and youth to provide opportunities for Bible study and discussion, worship and recreation, inspiration and song.

Youth-Team Ministry offers young people an opportunity to learn and grow in their Christian faith, as they assist congregations in their mission. International teams have been on every continent, involving young adults in a 15-month experience. National teams involve young adults over a two-year span of time, presenting musical concert programs in the United States and Canada. Spoke Folk is a two-week Bible camp experience. Youth age 16 and up bike approximately 50 miles per day, sharing programs and activities with congregations each day.

Christian Singles Conferences are weekend events for the divorced, widowed, or never married. Single adults from 18 on up gather for a weekend of learning, discussion, fellowship, and fun, gaining insights from well-known speakers from the Christian community.

LYE was incorporated in Minnesota in 1965 under the leadership of founder David Anderson. Rev. Larry Johnson has been president of LYE since 1973. Offices are located at 2500 39th Avenue NE, Minneapolis, Minnesota 55421-4284.

Lutheran Evangelism Association

The Lutheran Evangelism Association (LEvA) was organized in 1972 by the Rev. Erv Rasmussen, an LCMS clergyman, with the purpose of assisting Lutheran individuals and groups desiring to engage in personal evangelism.

The reader has already been introduced to a part of the ministry of the LEvA in the section on "Fair Ministry," one of the outreach methods of the organization.

The I'M HIS Partnership Witness Method is a Christ-centered Bible-based approach to witnessing. It is a simple program that can be used by itself or in conjunction with a visitation evangelism program. Each booklet and tract in the I'M HIS Partnership Witness Method have a return postcard or coupon, so that follow-up may take place with interested persons. The program requires consistent follow-up on the part of the witnessing Christian and invites the new Christian to witness to his or her Savior.

Prayer Family International is a nondenominational program of service through prayer and God's Word. Participants receive a biweekly Prayer Concern Letter, listing those prayer requests that readers have submitted. It contains articles on prayer, Bible studies, and other helpful information.

The Lutheran Fellowship of Andrew is a breakfast or supper group, which meets monthly or bimonthly over a meal to study together, pray together, and encourage one another in their witness. Witness methods and techniques are a part of the program at each gathering.

"Come, Let Us Reason Together" is a 15-minute radio program, utilizing a panel format to communicate the Gospel. An adult lay person, a teenager, and a pastor form the panel. Questions of Bible interpretation, discussion of the Christian life, the nature of the Gospel, and the like are a part of the program. Bible courses, Christian tracts, and booklets are offered to the listening audience.

The Phoenix Evangel is the publication of LEvA. It is designed to inform supporters and other interested individuals about the programs and materials of LEvA. LEvA has also sponsored Lutheran Evangelism Seminars.

Lutheran Evangelistic Movement

The Lutheran Evangelistic Movement (LEM) is an organization

committed to three major objectives:

1) Helping Christians to deepen their spiritual walk and live more effectively as disciples of Christ.

2) Bringing people of all ages to a personal commitment to Jesus Christ as Savior and Lord.

3) Equipping believers to use their gifts for the growth of the Body of Christ.[11]

A staff of one full-time director, Laurel M. Udden, and four part-time people coordinate several types of ministry, all of them intended to strengthen the evangelistic outreach of Christians. The Office of Resource Ministries offers an inventory of information and materials on methods of evangelism, evaluative tools for identifying the needs and strengths of the local church, and seminars on church growth and evangelism.

The Office of Youth Ministries recruits and trains young adults of the post high school age in music and drama in order to enable these young adults to carry on a ministry of youth-to-youth witness. Normally one team travels during the school year, and a couple of teams during the summer. Youth conferences are also a ministry of LEM.

These youth conferences are often planned in conjunction with area conferences. An area conference is a week of special meetings in a local congregation or among several congregations, something like the Preaching-Teaching-Reaching Missions of the 1950s or the open house services discussed later in this book. LEM provides speakers for these conferences.

LEM operates a year-round Evangel Retreat Center on Spring Lake near Dassel, Minnesota. It publishes a magazine called "Evangelize," in order to emphasize the importance of evangelism. It has a full-service Christian bookstore in Minneapolis, which offers the materials mentioned above.

LEM began in 1937 by providing speakers for the area conferences. It has continued to this day, operating under the banner of Lutheranism, but claiming no close affiliation with any particular Lutheran denomination. LEM is located at 833 2nd Ave. South, Minneapolis, Minnesota 55402.

Et Cetera

Many, many other evangelism ministries could be discussed in this chapter. The marketplace is as broad as the kinds of people within it. No book this size could possibly do justice to all of the evangelistic outreach programs which are designed to reach some special need in the marketplace. As an example of the extent to which this book could go, Kenneth Scott Latourette tells of a man named George Matheson, who began a mission in Shanghai to minister to the physical and spiritual needs of the ricksha pullers.[12] While this book is concentrating on the American scene, the illustration at least shows how detailed our subject could become.

Marketplace ministry has been done at the race track. It is being done among truck drivers. It has been done among families, fingered by the police, who have been frequently involved in domestic violence. It is being done among the elderly. It has been done among taxi cab drivers, oil field workers, migrant workers, and factory workers, cf. ERB, Book 13.

Find a group of people with some kind of identity, and someone undoubtedly has sought to share the Good News of salvation with them.

Resources

There are a few more resources that merit attention, in addition to those already covered, which will assist the Christian in reaching that rich man, poor man, beggar man, thief, doctor, lawyer, merchant, chief.

The *Evangelism Resource Book*, frequently cited on preceding pages, is valuable in its entirety, but Books 13, "Special Ministry," and 14, "Personal Evangelism Resources," are especially helpful for the marketplace. The "Word and Witness" program from the LCA attempts to equip Christians for witness through Bible study over an 18-month period of time. The small group setting is used for this. Filmstrips, cassette tapes, and reference materials are incorporated into the program.

"Witnesses for Christ" is a 10-week course from Augsburg, designed to motivate and equip people with the ability to verbalize the Gospel. A series of eight small booklets in the "My Witness Series," from the same source, talks about witness in special situations—in crisis situations, in the face of hostility, to those of another culture, etc. A leader's guide makes the booklets useful for teaching a series on witnessing.

The Lutheran Council in the U.S.A. (LCUSA) has produced some resources on apartment ministry. "Ten Things Your Congregation Can Do to Minister with Apartments' Residents" is a 16-page booklet, and "Apartment Dwellers" is a similar piece with much additional information. Write to the Lutheran Task Force on Apartment Ministry, 360 Park Avenue South, New York, New York 10010.

Chapter 6

The Mass Meeting Approach

The fourth chapter of this book has already covered the small-group approach, otherwise called the educational approach. This chapter will deal with the communication of the Gospel in the large group, in mass meetings—first those involving a single congregation and then those where several congregations band together for a joint effort.

The Book of Acts notes the various ways in which the rapid growth of the New Testament church occurred. There were personal testimonies of individual Christians (Acts 8:30-38), small group gatherings in homes (Acts 18), and evangelistic mission trips (Acts 15). Mass meetings in churches and public places (Acts 13) were also an important piece in this mosaic. Mass meetings can still serve the cause of Jesus Christ today, if they are seen as a *part* of our evangelistic work, never as ends in themselves. Mass meetings alone cannot effectively accomplish God's will to make disciples of all nations. What precedes and follows the mass meeting is crucial. The familiar story of Pentecost in Acts 2, itself the story of a mass meeting, illustrates the need for both preparation and follow-up. Much had taken place to prepare for that important event, and the results that followed have literally turned the world upside down.

Open House Services

It was an attitude of love and concern for lost souls that brought the mass meeting option to the attention of St. Mark's Lutheran Church,

Eureka, Missouri. They held their first series of meetings in 1975, and they have conducted these meetings annually since that time. During the first years, the LCMS Board for Evangelism stimulated this ministry at St. Mark's, as the Board tested the potential for reviving the Preaching-Teaching-Reaching Missions (PTR) of the 1950s and 60s. The Board subsequently developed materials for congregational use, calling this form of evangelism "Open House Services." The 10-step planning guidebook by Elmer Scheck, No. 1495, is published by Concordia.

The importance of follow-up after the services has become more evident each year. Pastor Darwin Karsten comments, "We have learned the need for nurture, follow-up, incorporation, and meeting the physical needs of people. It is important to involve new Christians in meaningful ministry within the congregation as soon as possible."

A committee under the congregation's Board of Evangelism begins planning at least eight months before the open house services. The committee seeks to involve as many people as possible in the planning process.

The work begins with much prayer by the committee and the congregation. Dates are selected for the services, and materials are written or gathered. Invitations, posters, tracts, letters for mass mailings, and other special items are needed. Various forms of advertising are used. The committee establishes a time schedule for visitation and for the mass mailings. Among the various themes St. Mark's has used for the week have been "Sharing the Love of Jesus Week." "Sharing Christ Week," "You Have a Friend—Jesus," and simply "Open House Services." The advertising and mailings emphasize the theme, and services and other special events also focus on it.

The special week begins with the Sunday morning worship services, followed by special services each evening, Sunday through Thursday. The services include special music, informal singing, the sharing of personal testimony, a children's message, Scripture readings, and responsive readings. A question and answer period has usually been included during the service time so that people have an opportunity to ask questions about various religious subjects and the teachings of the church. The services incorporate special times of prayer and an opportunity for people to respond to the speaker's message by coming to the altar. Occasional special emphasis nights focus on youth, the family, or some other group within the church or community. Special Bible studies take place during the weekday mornings and just prior to the evening services. These studies provide additional opportunities for people to grow spiritually during the week. If the meetings take place during the summer, some congregations may wish to coordinate them with Vacation Bible School.

The time of year selected for the open house services is entirely a matter of local choice. St. Mark's has tried various times with similar results. Each season can have its own benefits as well as its own drawbacks.

One of the key responsibilities of the organizing committee is to invite a guest speaker for the meetings and the Bible studies. Many members and visitors will be attracted by the speaker and his subject. St. Mark's has invited well-known evangelists, former seminary fieldworkers at St. Mark's who are now pastors elsewhere, and other speakers with special abilities in certain subject areas. The speaker's messages must be interesting, relevant, and evangelistic.

The organizing committee also recruits and arranges to train the people within the congregation who will be visiting and inviting others to the meetings. This training must have two important dimensions. First, people learn about the basics for witnessing to their faith in Christ. The witness workshop materials of the LCMS (covered earlier in this book) are one resource for that purpose. Second, members of the congregation are asked to invite friends, relatives, work and school associates, and other people with whom they have regular contact. Every age group can be involved in these invitations. "This approach has proven to be the most productive in involving visitors in the meetings," says Pastor Karsten.

Many positive spiritual blessings have resulted from the Open House ministry at St. Mark's Lutheran Church. People within the congregation have been enlightened about the need to reach the lost for Christ. Enthusiasm for the work of the Lord has increased. Spiritual growth has taken place among members through their involvement at the meetings and through their invitations to others. People who have been affected by this ministry have become anxious to invite their friends to these meetings.

During one evening service, a lady responded to the invitation at the end of the meeting. As she knelt at the altar, she confessed to the pastor a sin that had burdened her for years. Receiving the forgiveness of Christ during those moments, she later became an active disciple in the body of believers at St. Mark's.

For congregations considering this approach for their evangelistic ministry, Pastor Karsten offers seven important points:

1. It is only a *part* of your ministry, never an end in itself. It must be preceded by prayer, preparation, and planning, and it must be followed

by strong and continuous principles and programs of discipleship.

2. See it as a different thrust of your ministry. Make the meetings different in form and structure than your regular worship services. Include special music, children's messages and other methods of sharing the Gospel of Jesus Christ.

3. Invite a gifted evangelistic speaker, but do so early. Good speakers have busy schedules.

4. Involve the congregation in prayer for the meetings several months in advance and during the week of meetings. Challenge members to specific prayer for the speaker and for the people being invited.

5. Develop or gather helpful and appropriate materials for distribution. These materials could center on the special theme chosen for the week.

6. Register and welcome visitors by special recognition during the meetings, by name tags, or in some other way. Be sure to get their names and addresses for future follow-up.

7. Personally recruit people to be trained and involved. Involve as many of the congregation as possible in the planning and arrangements surrounding the meetings.

Several congregations, perhaps even an entire district or region, can participate in a joint open house venture. This allows for shared advertising and materials, mutual congregational encouragement, and meetings of the pastors and guest speakers for prayer, sharing, and Scripture study during the week of services.

Open House services enable active members to grow in their spiritual life. They revitalize the faith of inactive members and help to involve them in the life of the congregation. They introduce visitors to Jesus Christ and the joys and blessings of the Christian life.

Visitors' Sunday

A very simple but effective way to share the Gospel with a friend is for the Christian to invite that friend to a worship service. This is something that should happen every Sunday throughout the year, but sometimes a special emphasis reminds members of the importance of these invitations with the result that they make more of an effort to invite their friends and relatives to worship with them.

For example, on "Visitors' Sunday" at Mount Calvary Lutheran Church in Acton, Massachusetts, there were 50 visitors at the March 14, 1982 service. Fifty visitors is a lot, particularly for a church which averaged 210 worshipers in 1981.

Planning began months ahead of time, led by a committee of lay people in the congregation. Name tags in one color for members and another color for visitors were designed. The committee placed welcome cards in every pew and bulletin and asked visitors to fill out their names and addresses. They printed invitations for individual distribution. The Ongoing Ambassadors for Christ gave out invitations during their weekend in Acton the preceding month. Local advertising and news articles appeared in the newspapers. Eight hundred personalized Scriptures from the World Home Bible League were distributed March 7. People prayed for the event for months.

The 50 visitors on March 14 were warmly welcomed in church and invited to the post-service fellowship. More than 100 people had helped in some way to make "Visitors' Sunday" a success.

Follow-up calls were made on all visitors. "Since that time at least three of the families continue to worship at Mount Calvary," says Pastor Dennis Perryman. "It does not require a lot of training or a lot of money." It does require the willing participation of God's people, organization, and a willingness to invite friends, neighbors, and relatives to the worship services.[1]

When visitors come to our churches, it is imperative that they receive a warm welcome. One of the most important things that people look for in a Christian congregation is the love that sets Christians apart from other people. "A new command I give you: Love one another. As I have loved you, so you must love one another. All men will know that you are my disciples if you love one another" (John 13:34-35 NIV).

Sunny Beck wrote an article for *The Lutheran Witness* some years ago entitled "How Friendly is Your Church?" She and her husband spent a year traveling in a trailer, visiting 31 beautiful states, many friends and relatives, and 40 different Lutheran congregations. While they felt at home in the worship services, "Outside the church doors it was another story," she wrote. "We were appalled and saddened at the lack of communication. In only five congregations were we offered more than a handshake from the pastor; in only five did anyone show real interest in our being there."[2] Surely the love Jesus spoke of in John 13 should be expressed in the friendliness of Christian congregations to visitors.

"We can hear the objections now," she wrote. " 'But if we speak to people, we find they've been members longer than we.' (So perhaps you made some new friends that day.) 'No one speaks to us when we go to another church.' (That's sad, too.) 'We have a committee meeting right after church.' (Maybe all the committee members should be out there greeting with you.) 'The minister stands at the door.' (Good, but not enough.) 'We have a date to go to breakfast right after the service.' (You might invite the visitors to join you. Sometimes it's lonely in a strange city.)"³

Give all your visitors a warm, friendly welcome every Sunday, but in order to achieve that goal, it may be necessary to have a Visitors' Sunday once a year in order to direct members' attention to the importance of receiving visitors well. (Many congregations have introduced a "Moment of Fellowship" right after the sermon, during which time members and guests alike sign a visitors' register and greet one another. Other congregations have officially designated greeters, who make certain that no guest leaves unwelcomed.) After all, if no one ever visited your church, or if people visited but were never welcomed, your church would one day have to close its doors. The *Evangelism Resource Book* contains additional suggestions in Book 6. A. 1. b.

Miscellaneous

There are other ways in which the assembled congregation can be involved in an evangelistic ministry. C. Peter Wagner mentions a congregation in California that uses prayer as its only evangelism tool and does so with a great deal of success. Many denominations have something similar to an evangelism festival, as in the LCMS, where one Sunday each year evangelism is the focal point of the services. The sermon deals with evangelism, a banner proclaims the theme of the day, special liturgy ties the worship to the theme, and perhaps some type of congregational gathering occurs in the afternoon or evening. The evangelism festival could occur in conjunction with a Visitors' Sunday. A witness workshop could be scheduled for the afternoon and evening hours. The four-page resource folder, "Evangelism Catalog," from the Board for Evangelism Services of the LCMS, lists available materials for an evangelism festival, cf. ERB, Book 6. A. 3.

Most evangelistically minded people would insist that one Sunday a year is not enough. Preaching must be evangelistic every Sunday, in the sense that the Gospel is clearly communicated to the hearer. The LCA has put together a workshop for its clergy for the purpose of strengthening pastors in this area. The three-day program, entitled "Preaching From Commitment," concentrates on preaching, the relationship of preaching to the witness function, and the whole range of pastoral ministry. The workshop also covers the use of the narrative form in preaching.

An excellent resource from the LCA, which is useful for all Lutheran churches, is a brochure called "Worship and Witness." In the opening paragraph, the author notes,

> Worship in the parish can be a significant instrument of Evangelical Outreach. The implementation of our rich liturgical heritage, full celebration of the sacraments, meaningful preaching of the Word, worship leaders who are well-prepared and competent, worship space which is attractive and uncluttered, friendly people, good music—all of these can attract members and visitors alike to Sunday worship.[4]

Then the author leads the reader through a series of questions, enabling the reader to evaluate the effectiveness of his church in "Worship and Witness" in the following categories: building and worship space, publicity and evangelism, congregational climate, worship resources, Holy Baptism, Holy Communion, the service itself, and worship education. The questions indicate that there are many factors which affect the overall impression of the Sunday worship services. A meaningful worship experience is one of the most effective evangelistic tools a congregation has at its disposal.

For example, the reader rates his congregation on its "Congregational Climate" by answering five questions:

> Do greeters show hospitality and warmth to members and visitors alike?
> Are ushers warm and helpful to members and visitors alike?
> Do visitors and all members feel welcome at coffee hours?
> Are visitors greeted by fellow-worshipers before and after worship?
> Are persons of all ages and marital status made to feel a part of the congregation at worship?[5]

You can order this resource by writing the Division for Parish Services, Lutheran Church in America, 2900 Queen Lane, Philadelphia, Pennsylvania 19129, cf. also ERB, Book 6. A. 1.

Now let's take a look at mass-meeting evangelism *involving many congregations.* There are many well-known evangelists in the United States and abroad: James Robison of Texas, Bill Glass, Luis Palau of Argentina, Terry Winter of British Columbia, Bill McKee of Tempe, Arizona, etc. No modern-day evangelist, however, is better known or more highly respected than Billy Graham. For more than two decades the standard for mass evangelism has been the Billy Graham Crusades. While each evangelist is different and each crusade is conducted separately, most crusades have many points in common. Therefore, a look at a Billy Graham crusade will provide a glimpse at the workings of many other crusades as well.

The Billy Graham Evangelistic Association

Located at 1300 Harmon Place, Minneapolis, Minnesota 55403, the Billy Graham Evangelistic Association (BGEA) is a multifaceted organization with one goal, stated in its first Article of Incorporation: "To Spread the Gospel by Any and All Means...." While the crusade ministry is the most visible of its ministries, some attention should be paid to other aspects of the work of the organization.

World Wide Pictures has produced more than 120 films since its beginning in 1951. Every 15 minutes, one of its films is shown somewhere in the world. In 1981 more than 20 million people heard the Gospel through World Wide's evangelistic films.

Decision magazine has been in existence since 1962. It is now being published in 10 editions—four English editions, French, German, Spanish, Japanese, Chinese, and Braille. It is the main line of communication between the BGEA and its supporters. It appears monthly.

The Billy Graham Center at Wheaton, Illinois, is dedicated to the cause of evangelism and missions. A library of 50,000 volumes and 400 periodicals makes it a storehouse of information on these two subjects. An evangelistic film is shown at the end of every tour of the Center, and an invitation is given at the close of the film for people to take a spiritual step forward. More than 400 students were in attendance during the 1980-81 academic year, including 130 international students.

The World Emergency Fund is designated by donors for world emergencies in areas where natural disasters have struck, where refugees are in need, or where hunger and disease ravage the land.

The radio ministry ("Hour of Decision"), television broadcasts, telephone counseling, and counseling by mail are all extensions of the actual crusade ministry. In 1981 Billy Graham crusades were held in six cities: Mexico City, Mexico; Villahermosa, Mexico; Baltimore; San Jose; Houston; and Calgary, Alberta. In addition, 48 crusades were held during the year by nine associate evangelists: Akbar Abdul-Haqq, Ralph Bell, Robert Cunville, Roy Gustafson, Leighton Ford, Howard Jones, John Wesley White, Grady Wilson, and T. W. Wilson.

Held in conjunction with Billy Graham crusades, the Billy Graham School of Evangelism provides Bible studies, evangelism lectures, inspirational addresses, and seminars designed to strengthen the leadership of the local congregation in the work of evangelism. Students, pastors, and lay people attend these four- and five-day schools. Under the leadership of Dr. Kenneth Chafin, Dean of the School, over 70,000 have attended these schools during the years since they began in 1962.

Years of preparation must precede any Billy Graham crusade.

Leadership committees must be formed, offices rented, churches enlisted for their support, budgets raised, counselors trained, prayers offered, and publicity carried out.

When the crusade takes place, the special choirs and singers, the testimonies of prominent Christians, the messages of the evangelist, and the moment when people are invited to come forward at the conclusion of the service—all this is the consummation of thousands of hours and many months of hard work. The bottom line of crusade evangelism is usually reported as the number in attendance and the number of decisions recorded.

A closer look at and critique of the evangelistic crusade follows, based upon the information and insights of Dr. Win Arn of the Institute for American Church Growth. A study was done on the Greater Seattle Crusade by the Institute one year after that 1976 crusade, which was described as the "...most exciting and successful U.S. Billy Graham crusade in years."[6]

In his report on the results of the study, Dr. Arn has suggested that effective evangelism is to be measured by the number of people discipled and incorporated into the church, not in the number of people who made a decision. As reported earlier, he has applied the same criterion to the "Here's Life" campaign. In order to determine how many of those who made decisions were incorporated into a Christian church one year later, 1,200 pastors were polled in the Greater Seattle / Tacoma area.

Arn learned that among the follow-up cards received by those churches, 30.6 percent indicated that the person filling out the card had become a Christian, 53.7 percent indicated that the person was already a Christian, but was rededicating his life to Christ, and 15.7 percent of the follow-up cards were filled out for unknown reasons. Arn suggests that mass evangelism in many cases might be more accurately called "mass revival."[7]

Pastors were asked, "As a direct result of the crusade, how many are now (one year later) new members of your church?" From a total of 434,100 persons who attended the crusade, there were 18,136 who came forward at Graham's invitation. Of that 18,316, slightly more than seven percent were members of a local church one year later.[8]

In order to accomplish more effective mass evangelism, Arn makes six suggestions:
1. Change the goal from registering decisions to "making disciples and responsible members of the church."
2. Precede each crusade with adequate church growth training for pastors and key lay leaders.

3. Elevate the importance of the local church in mass evangelism.
4. Encourage and train laity to evangelize.
5. Develop and utilize natural bridges of evangelism through friends and relatives.
6. Structure a year-round strategy of effective evangelism in participating local churches.[9]

Many positive benefits come from mass evangelism. People do become Christians. Christians learn how better to share their faith. The name of Jesus Christ is publicly and widely proclaimed. Churches grow. However, the analysis of the Institute for American Church Growth suggests that mass evangelism can be done more effectively.

Some of the same theological concerns raised earlier could also be raised here. An emphasis upon the grace of God at work to convert a sinner to faith in Christ would be far preferable to an emphasis upon man's "decision" to accept Christ.

Lutheran Hour Rallies

Lutheran Hour rallies have been held in the LCMS for many years. Although such rallies have not had evangelistic goals in the past, there has recently been added an outreach emphasis known as the "Added Dimension." Traditionally, Lutheran Hour rallies have been rallies by Lutherans in support of the Lutheran Hour and the Lutheran Laymen's League (LLL).

After a request for a rally comes from the sponsoring area, the LLL helps the area churches to form a Steering Committee, secure the support of the local LCMS clergy and churches, select a rally committee, rally site, rally date, rally speaker, etc. All of the necessary plans for financial support, printing, and other arrangements are done by the local people with the assistance of the LLL Coordinator of Rallies.

The purpose of the "Added Dimension" is to make a special effort to invite the public, as well as inactive church members, to the rally. The program includes several "Evenings of Inspiration" that are held in congregations in the rally site area prior to the actual rally. People who attend the "Evenings of Inspiration" are encouraged to invite their friends and neighbors to the rally so that they may hear the Gospel preached and have opportunity to respond to that message.

Counselors are trained to speak with people who respond to the evangelistic appeal that is given. Response is noted on a special "May We Help You" card and followed up by trained evangelists from the community churches during the weeks after the rally. A witness workshop is held as a part of the training for lay people.

One such Lutheran Hour rally was held on Sunday afternoon, October 17, 1982, in the civic auditorium of Omaha, Nebraska. After two years of planning from the local rally committee, the Rev. Wallace Schulz, associate Lutheran Hour speaker, and the Rev. W. Leroy Biesenthal, Associate Secretary for Evangelism for the Board for Evangelism Services of the LCMS, arrived one week before the rally to begin the "Added Dimension."

They conducted nearly a dozen "Evenings of Inspiration" in the area. These evenings of Bible study and song were supplemented by a special prayer service on the eve of the rally. On Friday, Rev. Biesenthal conducted workshops for area pastors and trained about 70 counselors for follow-up. On Saturday, he led a witness workshop for lay people. That same day nearly 100 youth helped distribute thousands of brochures, inviting people to the rally.

During the week Rev. Schulz spoke to various Christian day schools in the area and held radio and newspaper interviews. A special press conference was held with the mayor of Omaha, who proclaimed October 17 Lutheran Hour Rally Sunday in Omaha.

The musical talents of bands and choirs added much to the rally, which was taped for television viewing at a later time. The choir included 700 adults and 500 children. Rev. Schulz based his message on Hebrews 12, encouraging people to "fix their eyes on Jesus," so they might not lose heart in life. The cards filled out in response to the message revealed a variety of needs—loneliness, desperation, depression, and the like. Many inquirers expressed a desire to learn how to study the Bible effectively.[10]

In order to request a Lutheran Hour rally for your area with the "Added Dimension," write to the International Lutheran Laymen's League, 2185 Hampton Ave., St. Louis, Missouri 63139, ATTN: Coordinator of Rallies.

Miscellaneous

Other multi-congregational mass evangelism efforts could be discussed on these pages. Some of the most prominent evangelists in America have been mentioned only briefly in this chapter. The mass evangelistic efforts of the "Here's Life, America" campaign have been covered in the section on Campus Crusade for Christ. Still other possibilities for this type of outreach exist, limited only by the imagination of the human mind.

The same is true for every chapter of this book. By the time these pages are published, they will already be somewhat obsolete.

Evangelism approaches and programs arise, change, and develop as people use them, evaluate them, and revise them.

This author has sought to put down on paper some concrete ideas and suggestions within the broad strokes of timeless evangelistic approaches—through visitation, by way of the U.S. mail, on the high school or college campus, in the small group at the church or in the Christian home, out in the marketplace, and at the local church as it gathers together to worship or as it gathers together with many churches to worship. It is hoped that the approaches, programs, and resources on these pages will stimulate individuals and congregations to greater evangelistic activity with the result that many more people will come to believe that Jesus died on the cross for their salvation.

Notes

Introduction

1. You may contact the International Lutheran Laymen's League (LLL), 2185 Hampton Ave., St. Louis, Missouri 63139, for some assistance in this area. Another fine resource is Book 15 of the *Evangelism Resource Book* (ERB), published by Concordia Publishing House (CPH), No. 9-2399, Erwin J. Kolb, editor.

Chapter 1

1. Kent R. Hunter, "Ongoing Ambassadors for Christ: An Objective Analysis Based on Comprehensive Research with Recommendations for the Improvement of This Important Ministry (An Abbreviated Report)" (Detroit: The Church Growth Analysis and Learning Center, 1980), p. 2.
2. Cf. ERB, Book 10.E.6.
3. Cf. "Evangelism Catalog," p. 4, No. 1370, and other helps.
4. D. James Kennedy, *Evangelism Explosion*, revised edition (Wheaton, Illinois: Tyndale House Publishers, 1977), Appendix A, pp. 186-98.
5. W. Leroy Biesenthal, *Dialog Evangelism* (St. Louis: The Board for Evangelism, The Lutheran Church—Missouri Synod, n.d.), p. 4.
6. Donald A. Abdon, *Organizing Around the Great Commission* (Indianapolis: Parish Leadership Seminars, Inc., 1977), Introduction.
7. Alan Harre, "Criteria for Evaluation in the Church," *Issues in Christian Education* 15 (Summer 1981), pp. 14-18.
8. Kennedy, *Evangelism Explosion*, p.2.
9. Arthur E. Graf, *The Church in the Community: An Effective Evangelism Program for the Christian Congregation* (Grand Rapids: William B. Eerdmans Publishing Company, 1965), pp. 12-14.
10. Kennedy, *Evangelism Explosion*, p. 177.
11. Ibid., p. 70.
12. Ibid., pp. 42, 67-68.
13. Ibid., p. 69.
14. Ibid., pp. 118-22.

Chapter 2

1. Walter Mueller, *Direct Mail Seminar: Study Guide & Manual* (Maple Glen, Pennsylvania: Specialized Ministries Center, 1978), p. 39

Chapter 3

1. "The Navigators: Annual Report 1981" (Colorado Springs, Colorado: The Navigators, 1981), p. 2.
2. The Navigators brochure (Colorado Springs, Colorado: The Navigators, n.d.).
3. "Inter-Varsity 1: Student Leadership," revised edition (Madison, Wisconsin: Inter-Varsity Christian Fellowship, 1982), p. 5.
4. Ibid., p. 190.
5. J. D. Douglas, ed., *Let The Earth Hear His Voice: International Congress on World Evangelization* (Minneapolis: World Wide Publications, 1975), p. 4.
6. "Helping People Reach People, 30 Years: 1981 Annual Report, Campus Crusade for Christ, Inc." (San Bernardino, CA: Campus Crusade for Chirst, Inc., 1981), p. 13.
7. Win Arn, "A Church Growth Look at.... Here's Life America" in *The Pastor's Church Growth Handbook* (Pasadena: Church Growth Press, 1979), pp. 58-59.
8. Ibid., pp. 46-56.
9. Fellowship of Christian Athletes brochure (Kansas City, Missouri: Fellowship of Christian Athletes, n.d.), p. 8.
10. Ibid., p. 2.
11. Oscar Schisgall, "Tomorrow Is in Their Hands," *The Saturday Evening Post* 247 (October 1975), pp. 22-23. Reprinted with permission from The Saturday Evening Post Company, 1975.
12. Young Life "Purpose" brochure (Colorado Springs, Colorado: Young Life, n.d.).
13. James C. Hefley, *God Goes to High School* (Waco, Texas: Word Books, 1970), p. 40.

Chapter 4

1. "Evangelism Through Schools," *The Evangel-Gram* 4 (September 1982), p. 5.
2. "Evangelism Training in Third Grade," *The Evangel-Gram* 2 (December 1980), pp. 4-5.
3. Charles Arn, Donald McGavran, Win Arn, *Growth: A New Vision for the Sunday School* (Pasadena: Church Growth Press, 1980), p. 33.
4. "Child Evangelism Fellowship" Brochure (Warrenton, Missouri: Child Evangelism Fellowship, Inc.), p. 1.
5. Marilyn Kunz, "Bible Studies that Bring Them to Belief," *Christianity Today* 25 (October 2, 1981), pp. 20-23.
6. Dorothy Naumann, " 'Reach Out' on Tape," *The Evangel-Gram* 4 (March 1982), p. 2.

Chapter 5

1. " 'Reach Out' at the Fair," *The Evangel-Gram* 3 (March 1982), p. 3.
2. Edward A. Schmidt, "Special Ministry," Book 13 of the *Evangelism Resource Book*, Section C, "Ministry to Vacationers" (St. Louis: Concordia Publishing House, 1980), p. 4.
3. Kathy Sandor, "Remember Those Who Are in Prison," *The Evangel-Gram* 2 (September 1980), pp. 4-5; Allen D. Hanson, "Christian Prison Visitation," *The Evangel-Gram* 2 (September 1981), p. 5; Allen D. Hanson, "Four Ministries in One," *The Evangel-Gram* 3 (March 1982), p. 8.
4. "Prison Fellowship: 1981 Annual Report" (Washington, D.C.: Prison Fellowship, 1982), p. 8.
5. "Hands that Lift: There Is Hope!" brochure (High Ridge, Missouri: Teen Challenge St. Louis, n.d.).
6. David Manuel, Jr., with Donald Wilkerson and Reginald Yake, *The Jesus Factor* (Plainfield, New Jersey: Logos International, 1977), back cover.
7. "Hands that Lift: There Is Hope!" brochure.
8. Randy Frame, "Jews for Jesus to Begin 'Y'shua' Ad Campaign," *Christianity Today* 26 (November 26, 1982), p. 58.
9. Ibid., p. 60.

10. Lutheran Youth Encounter brochure (Minneapolis: Lutheran Youth Encounter, n.d.).
11. "A Resource for a Growing Church" brochure (Minneapolis: Lutheran Evangelistic Movement, n.d.).
12. Kenneth Scott Latourette, *A History of the Expansion of Christianity*, vol. 6: *The Great Century: North Africa and Asia* (Grand Rapids: Zondervan Publishing House, 1970), p. 346.

Chapter 6

1. "Company Is Coming!" *The Evangel-Gram* 4 (September 1982), p. 1.
2. Sunny Beck, "How Friendly Is Your Church?" *The Lutheran Witness* 99 (February 1979), p. 10.
3. Ibid., p. 11.
4. "Worship and Witness" brochure (Philadelphia: Division for Parish Services, n.d.), p. 1.
5. Ibid., p. 2.
6. *Decision* (August 1976), cited in Win Arn, "Mass Evangelism: The Bottom Line" in *The Pastor's Church Growth Handbook* (Pasadena: Church Growth Press, 1979), p. 98.
7. Ibid., p. 100.
8. Ibid.
9. Ibid., pp. 105-109.
10. "Rallying to Support the Lutheran Hour and Reaching Out to Bring Christ to Our Nation," *BCTN Magazine* (December 1982), pp. 8-9.

Bibliography

Abdon, Donald A. *Organizing Around the Great Commission.* Indianapolis: Parish Leadership Seminars, Inc., 1977.
Arn, Charles; McGavran, Donald; and Arn, Win. *Growth: A New Vision for the Sunday School.* Pasadena: Church Growth Press, 1980.
Arn, Win. "A Church Growth Look at...Here's Life America." In *The Pastor's Church Growth Handbook*, pp. 44-60. Edited by Win Arn. Pasadena: Church Growth Press, 1979.
Arn, Win. "Mass Evangelism: The Bottom Line." In *The Pastor's Church Growth Handbook*, pp. 95-109. Edited by Win Arn. Pasadena: Church Growth Press, 1979.
Beck, Sunny. "How Friendly Is Your Church?" *The Lutheran Witness* 99 (February 1979), pp. 10-11.
Biesenthal, W. Leroy. *Dialog Evangelism.* St. Louis: The Board for Evangelism, The Lutheran Church—Missouri Synod, n.d.
"Company Is Coming!" *The Evangel-Gram* 4 (September 1982), p. 1.
Douglas, J. D., ed. *Let the Earth Hear His Voice: International Congress on World Evangelization.* Minneapolis: World Wide Publications, 1975.
"Evangelism Catalog." St. Louis: The Board for Evangelism Services, The Lutheran Church—Missouri Synod, n.d.
"Evangelism Through Schools." *The Evangel-Gram* 4 (September 1982), p. 5.
"Evangelism Training In Third Grade." *The Evangel-Gram* 2 (December 1980), pp. 4-5.
Frame, Randy. "Jews for Jesus to Begin 'Y'shua' Ad Campaign." *Christianity Today* 26 (November 26, 1982), pp. 58-60.
Graf, Arthur E. *The Church in the Community: An Effective Evangelism Program for the Christian Congregation.* Grand Rapids: William B. Eerdmans Publishing Company, 1965.
Hanson, Allen D. "Four Ministries in One." *The Evangel-Gram* 3 (March 1982), p. 8.
_____. "Christian Prison Visitation." *The Evangel-Gram* 2 (September 1982), p. 5.

Harre, Alan. "Criteria for Evaluation in the Church." *Issues in Christian Education* 15 (Summer 1981), pp. 14-18.

Hefley, James C. *God Goes to High School*. Waco, Texas: Word Books, 1970.

"Helping People Reach People, 30 Years: 1981 Annual Report, Campus Crusade for Christ, Inc." San Bernardino, California: Campus Crusade for Christ, Inc., 1981.

Hunter, Kent R. "Ongoing Ambassadors for Christ: An Objective Analysis Based on Comprehensive Research with Recommendations for the Improvement of This Important Ministry (An Abbreviated Report)." Detroit: The Church Growth Analysis and Learning Center, 1980.

"Inter-Varsity 1: Student Leadership." Revised edition. Madison, Wisconsin: Inter-Varsity Christian Fellowship, 1982.

Kennedy, D. James. *Evangelism Explosion*. Revised edition. Wheaton, Illinois: Tyndale House Publishers, 1977.

Kolb, Erwin J., ed. *Evangelism Resource Book*. St. Louis: Concordia Publishing House, 1980.

Kunz, Marilyn. "Bible Studies that Bring Them to Belief." *Christianity Today* 25 (October 2, 1981), pp. 20-23.

Latourette, Kenneth Scott. *A History of the Expansion of Christianity*. Vol. 6: *The Great Century: North Africa and Asia*. Grand Rapids: Zondervan Publishing House, 1970.

Manuel, David, Jr.; with Wilkerson, Donald, and Yake, Reginald. *The Jesus Factor*. Plainfield, New Jersey: Logos International, 1977.

Mueller, Walter. *Direct Mail Seminar: Study Guide & Manual*. Maple Glen, Pennsylvania: Specialized Ministries Center, 1978.

Naumann, Dorothy. " 'Reach Out' on Tape." *The Evangel-Gram* 3 (March 1982), p. 2.

"The Navigators: Annual Report 1981." Colorado Springs, Colorado: The Navigators, 1981.

"Prison Fellowship: 1081 Annual Report." Washington, D.C.: Prison Fellowship, 1982.

"Rallying to Support the Lutheran Hour and Reaching Out to Bring Christ to Our Nation." *BCTN Magazine* (December 1982), pp. 8-9.

" 'Reach Out' at the Fair." *The Evangel-Gram* 3 (March 1982), p. 3.

Sandor, Kathy, "Remember Those Who Are in Prison." *The Evangel-Gram* 2 (September 1980), pp. 4-5.

Schisgall, Oscar. "Tomorrow Is in Their Hands." *The Saturday Evening Post* 247 (October 1975), pp. 22-24.